COAL
AND THE
COAST

COAL AND THE COAST

A reflection on the
PIKE RIVER
DISASTER

PAUL MAUNDER

ᘮᑎ

CANTERBURY UNIVERSITY PRESS

UNIVERSITY OF
CANTERBURY
Te Whare Wānanga o Waitaha
CHRISTCHURCH NEW ZEALAND

First published in 2012
CANTERBURY UNIVERSITY PRESS
University of Canterbury
Private Bag 4800, Christchurch
NEW ZEALAND
www.cup.canterbury.ac.nz

Text copyright © 2012 Paul Maunder
Photographs copyright © the photographers as named

The moral rights of the author and photographers have been
asserted.

ISBN 978-1-927145-26-5

A catalogue record for this book is available from the
National Library of New Zealand.

Cover photo: Flames burn out of control from a ventilation shaft at
the Pike River mine on 30 November 2010.
Iain McGregor-Pool/Getty Images

Back cover painting: *The Start of Summer 2010*, by Alison Hale

Book design and layout: Quentin Wilson, Christchurch
Printed by PrintStop, Wellington

CONTENTS

ACKNOWLEDGEMENTS

Thanks to Ray Richards for suggesting I write the book, to Eva Brown for being a first and very expert reader, to Rachel Scott for her warm welcome to Canterbury University Press and for making some crucial suggestions. I also acknowledge the team at Theatre and Film Studies, Peter Falkenberg and Sharon Mazer, who have, over the last few years, stimulated some ageing grey matter. Finally, to Caroline, for her support on all fronts.

The One and the Many

(And it's okay to skip this bit!)

This book is written with a consciousness informed by the French philosopher Alain Badiou. Badiou, a postmarxist, bases his thought on set theory, the theory through which school children now learn their maths.[2]

1st set	2nd set	3rd set
0	V	C
0	V	C
0	V	C
etc		

If you draw the sets together, the areas that overlap become areas of *multiplicity*, that is, areas where singular characteristics co-exist.

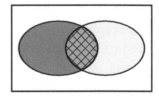

Take a worksite and construct the sets: men, women, Pākehā, Māori, Pacific Islander, heterosexual, gay, different age groups and so on. At work, all these sets overlap to varying degrees. Similarly, analyse a church, a school, a family … The model fits well a world characterised by diversity.

But is there some direction behind this diversity, or are people governed only by individual desire for material comfort? This would be the neo-liberal[3] belief. In which case identity politics has simply resulted in an increasingly diverse marketplace – you can buy kava as well as tea at the local dairy.

For Badiou, however, diversity creates 'immanent unfolding of being as inconsistent multiplicity' – a daunting phrase. But it is able to be unpacked, for it is how we experience things. Badiou is saying that my being – that which I think of as 'me' – continues to unfold within myself in terms of the elements that make me what I am (man, writer, partner, citizen, father, Pākehā …). These elements are not altogether integrated or consistent. That's fair enough. The writer can be at odds with the citizen, the father at odds with the partner, and so on. As well, according to the situation, the set characteristic may change: being a man might well mean one thing at the playcentre, and another in the rugby team.

In addition, this 'individuality as inconsistent multiplicity' is entwined with 'community and society as inconsistent multiplicity', for a set that is an element of me as individual is also a collective set (males, Pākehā etc), and the same rules apply at this level. The idea of being male is constantly evolving, with variable ideas within the set of males …

But because of the 'unfolding', Badiou holds on to a sense of an evolving world – the 'better world is possible' of the traditional Marxists. This unfolding is much more complex than the traditional view, which was characterised by a singular working class leading a singular revolution.

Instead, for Badiou, late capitalism as an imperial force promotes a singular world-view and can only be confronted from the basis of multiplicity. The problem, of course, is that the multiplicity is inconsistent and this leads to a confused response. But during events that occur at specific sites, and which are characterised by conditions of excess and scarcity, its underlying coherence is seen more clearly, and the future – the better world – is momentarily revealed.

The task of the commentator, then, is to construct the means to express, if only for an instant, the possible future toward which we stumble. This involves naming the event – that is, choosing a word or words that define, in the same way that we 'name' a new child, taking into account the family background, the birth, the place of birth, and so on. There can be conflict over the name. The child may go without a name for a time. This complex task of naming can resonate more widely, for example: what were the consequences of the failure of the Copenhagen Climate Change Talks?

For Badiou, the epoch we live in is made up of ruptures and continuities that cannot easily be captured, but during an *event*, being unfolds in a more consistent way.

This book presents the Pike River disaster within Badiou's difficult, but for me hopeful, framework.

We must set apart a place for memory, for history,
for that mirror which reminds us who we were,
shows us what we are and promises
what we may become.

– Subcomandante Marcos,
Zapatista Army of National Liberation,
Mexico.[1]

The Shape of Coal

Blackball, the place where I live, has evolved from a coalmining town of close to 2000 people in the 1940s, to a village of 350, containing a diversity of people: some old-timers, some transients, a mix of people commuting to a variety of jobs, a few self-employed, a few beneficiaries, and a growing number of Filipino women. There is a tourist hotel, 'Formerly The Blackball Hilton', salami and honey factories, some holiday homes, and motorcycle and vintage car clubs regularly visit.

As in all towns on the West Coast the infrastructure is fragile, but a Sky or Freeview disc graces most houses and broadband gives access to the digital world of information and social networking. Cellphone reception, however, is poor. There is no middle class in Blackball. Instead, an underclass lurks on the edge of poverty and the occasional small dope crop grows in the surrounding forest.

In this time of increasingly frequent natural disasters, the village feels well situated, protected by the surrounding hills from tornadoes, safe on its plateau from floods and tsunamis, well drained by a network of ditches, and the rock-filled earth on which it is built would be stable enough in an earthquake.

I often go for a walk out of town, past a substantial two-storey villa in need of restoration, once the mine manager's house and now a community centre. As I leave the plateau the temperature drops. Alongside the road is a bank of rock in which narrow seams of black coal stretch horizontally. It reminds me of Thomas Brunner, the first white man to be made aware of the Paparoa coal deposits, and his epic journey from Nelson through the Buller Gorge to the Coast. It was a rain-bedevilled adventure that almost killed him and certainly shortened his life. This is Gondwanaland and there is a different, harsher spirit to the land, fostering the same awareness of the ancient that I felt in Africa.

On the left, the road falls away to a creek bed and it is difficult now to imagine the railway station that used to sit there, together with shunting yards and coal bins. On the right, the rectangle of brick walls was once the bathhouse, which served not only the miners at the end of their shift but the wider town. Kids would be taken there for a weekly scrub, as would visiting league teams at the end of a match.

After turning off the road and walking up a hill for a hundred metres I am at the original Blackball mine site, indicated by two ventilation chimneys and the remnants of the steam-driven fan. Down to the left is the blocked-up portal of the mine, leading to the huge network of now flooded tunnels that lie under the village. The Blackball mine was wet and sulphurous and the continued runoff of leachate into the creek has killed all life in the water.

It is a relatively recent ruin, and there are people still alive in the village who worked here, who remember a town of many shops with a taxi service and weekly movies in the miners' hall, with sports teams and a policeman, and a doctor employed by the union. They remember the pick and banjo shovel days and the characters of an era rich in nostalgia, fertile territory for a writer to explore – a romance? Similar ruins, similar stories, similar romances dot the Coast.

But this book is not another romance. I am, instead, trying to perceive the future by putting context to an event, the Pike River coalmine disaster of 2010, which killed 29 men, and to explore its implications.

As I stand on the old mine site and breathe in the atmosphere, fantails hover and dart, a weka forages and a kereru heavily thumps past. It is about to rain. Nature is indifferent to stories of the past, to romance, to nostalgia, even to the future.

Turning to go back home, I remember what first brought me to this place.

In 1997, towards the end of the neo-liberal 'revolution' in New Zealand, I collaborated with Sue Bradford and members of the Auckland Unemployed Workers' Rights Centre to produce a recent history of Aotearoa from the point of view of the unemployed. We toured the play nationally and did a gig at the Blackball Hilton. For a pub performance it was a remarkably focused audience and afterwards I noticed an old banner on the wall featuring the words 'Solidarity For Ever' – an unusual wall-hanging in a commercial establishment.

I continued to return to Blackball to celebrate Mayday, which, as an event, had disappeared from the rest of the country. I discovered the story of the pub, which proprietor Jane Wells and her business partner had jokingly called the Blackball Hilton, only to receive a threatening letter from the American Hilton chain, which intended to sue. In a flash of inspiration they changed the name to Formerly The Blackball Hilton – one of the cheekier community victories over the multinationals.

But I also discovered the story of the 1908 Blackball strike and its catalytic effect on working-class political development. The village, in fact, seemed to be a shrine, and as I began to discover the wider Coast, the region felt something of a tūrangawaewae for a person of working-class origins. Many Pākehā have this reaction: part reality, part nostalgia.

The Coast has a complex genealogy, with each family member contributing a different culture, all of them (apart from farming and tourism) based on extraction (and sometimes, even farming and tourism can seem like extractive industries).

The Māori extracted pounamu, with the stone being one of the centres of founding mythology. And then the gold-diggers arrived, flamboyant individualists who could inspire and destroy a town in days, leaving a legacy of tailings, so that any creek bed, while posing as natural, is in fact man-made. Coalmining followed and bred a particular kind of camaraderie. Barbara Freese, in her illuminating study of the history of coal, writes of 'the unique mixture of awe, sympathy, guilt and fear that these workers [coalminers] have long inspired. It comes from their work in that most mysterious and dangerous of places, the deep underground, and from their distinctive and isolated tight-knit communities.'[4]

Canterbury historian Len Richardson considers that New Zealand coalmining communities became centres of radicalism in the early 20th century because of their isolation, which held intact the union traditions brought by the migrant workers from Britain. In urban areas the traditions were diluted by the possibilities of self-employment and land ownership.[5]

More recently, dairy farming and tourism have developed modern industries guided by managerialism and dependent on sustainability, sometimes in conflict with the extractive industries, and breeding a different sort of worker.

Behind all of these genealogical strands is the extremity of the rainforest climate, temperate but wet, and the complex and aged landscape.

As a region the Coast retains, therefore, the characteristics of a Third World province, with global capital arriving to extract resources and take them elsewhere to add value. Boom-and-bust cycles are then inevitable.

The current population consists mainly of working-class people who also hunt and gather, are sometimes eccentric and reclusive, wary of the bureaucrat, and in some eyes feral. But there are as well the alternative lifestylers, often from other countries: Britain, Germany or the US, and a growing ethnic diversity: black Zimbabwean or Kenyan farm labourers, even sharemilkers ... Accordingly, in this book I will avoid the 'homely' portrayal of the Coast as a pubful of Barry Crump 'characters', and instead portray the people in their true variety.

The trigger for this book has been the Pike River disaster. The recounting of my personal response to this event (Chapter 1) will lead to a potted history of coal on the Coast – its economic structure as an industry, the early workers, the historical changes they helped trigger and their contribution to the formation of New Zealand society (Chapter 2). From there the book proceeds to the continuing question of worker safety and the economic and legislative structures required to achieve it (Chapter 3). Then I return to the political narrative, examining changes since the closure of many pits in the 1960s, and the betrayals the people of the Coast feel the region has experienced since then (Chapter 4). Climate change and the role of New Zealand-produced coal in the 21st century, as well as issues of sustainability and how this issue may be played out locally, are the subject of Chapter 5. I move to defining the modern miner and the values that drive such a person. If they are newcomers, what has brought them to the Coast? Has there been a fundamental change or is there continuity (Chapter 6)? Finally, what image, what new knowledge, what guidelines for the future has writing about this event produced (Chapter 7)?

As I enter the village again, a coal truck and trailer unit rumbles past, the driver staring ahead watchfully. School is out for the day and the kids are circulating through the village on their bikes. The mine at Roa still operates, washing out high-value coking coal for the European market.

A pile of logs lies on Scottie's lawn, ready to be cut up for firewood. People around here don't do things by halves – a bag of wood from an urban service station is ludicrous in comparison, and every self-respecting male has a chainsaw. Young Sean and his mate, both five-year-olds, yell their way down the main road on their bikes. For a moment they own the road and there are no anxious mothers in sight. They will evolve onto trail bikes by the age of eight and will be boy racers by the age of 16. If they survive that period, they will turn into young men who shed a tear as their partner gives birth.

Or maybe by then they will have gone to Aussie.

I arrive home to be greeted by the hens. I toss the food into their pen and wait for them to fearfully skirt around me before I shut the gate. Their paranoia is entirely unreasonable.

And as resolute as all natural processes.

CHAPTER ONE

The Unfolding Event

The Pike River mine, which is located 12 kilometres north of Blackball, exploded at 3.44pm on Friday 19 November 2010. Of the 18 miners and 13 contractors in the mine only two survived, and for a week the world's media focused on the Coast, for it was the biggest collective loss of life in this country since the 1979 Air New Zealand Erebus crash.

In Badiou's framework, the onset of a disaster constitutes a 'rupture' in the normal flow of daily life. There are any number of subjective views in the first moments of an event, with chance encounters, rumours and opinions impinging. These subjective flows are initially private, or perhaps incompletely shared with immediate family or colleagues. Soon the media will be hunting them out and placing them in a new context. Eventually they will become more objectified, through official inquiries of one sort or another, perhaps leading to legislative change, but with the overall intent of returning to the status quo.

That November, encountering this unfolding event, I kept a diary for a few days,[6] and begin the 'naming' of this event with my own subjective view.

Day One: Friday 19 November 2010

Late in the afternoon it looks like rain, so I decide to mow the lawns. At this time of the year you can pause and see the grass growing. I get as far as the roadside verge when the ambulance, siren blaring, exits from the station rooms and heads toward me. It comes to a halt and Larrie tells me to get in. 'Explosion at Pike River.' I race inside for my boots and uniform.

As we drive through Moonlight, I think back to the afternoon three years ago when, as part of the Runanga School centennial celebrations, I recorded on video a dozen or so members of the mines rescue team and relatives of workers killed in the Strongman mine disaster of 1967. They'd come together and remembered 'that fateful day', as one of them called it: the news disseminating, the rescue team going in, the waiting, the misunderstandings, the knock on the door ... An explosion in a mine is a terrible thing and the recording was a tearful occasion.

We turn off the main road and drive through dairy farms to the control gates of the mine. Pike River, like all industrial complexes in rural settings, has a surreal feeling, particularly strong in this case as the mine is discreetly nestled in national park beech forest. A creek rattles beside the narrow road, alongside which the coal is carried as a slurry in two pipes, and weka peck in the garden outside the office blocks.

We join the row of ambulances and are divided into teams, assigned numbers and leaders and equipment. Suddenly a 4WD arrives and two men are led out, covered in coal dust, a whiter scale around their eyes and mouth where tears and saliva have mixed with the coal. 'Where am I?' one of them mutters. 'Was there an explosion?' He is confused as I help lead him into an ambulance.

There is no further action, other than a further rescue helicopter arriving from Nelson and grim-faced managers striding between meetings. The ambulance leaves, carrying the two survivors to hospital. But 29 men remain down there. Banal conversations take place and hunger bites – it is past teatime. The mayor is here as part of the fire crew and in a whispered conversation we agree that the men below are probably dead.

Already the question begins to hover: Given modern equipment, how could such a thing happen? I remember one of our interviewees analysing Strongman: lax practices had crept in and shortcuts had become common practice. Pike is a gassy mine, as the area is complex geologically and they've had to tunnel through an extensive fault-line of broken rock. There have been a string of delays in developing the infrastructure, leading to budget overruns.

It begins to rain and we have to shift under shelter. The boredom grows and I regret mowing the lawns and thus being noticed. War must be like this: 90 per cent boredom, officers trying to make sense of chaos, sparse information, interspersed with moments of sheer terror … I go and make a cup of tea. A middle-aged man, in shock, sits staring straight ahead. He tells me he was driving down into the mine and the motor of his vehicle started to cut out. Not enough oxygen. He turned around and made it to safety.

Pizzas arrive and the hunger is assuaged, but nothing else is happening. The Nelson crew leave in their chopper. Eventually we locals are stood down as well. The rescue team won't be going in tonight. This seems odd. I remember at Strongman they went in straight away, established a fresh-air base, then started to penetrate further.

We drive back to Blackball, drop our paperwork in to the ambulance manager's house and see that the names of the Blackball men who work at Pike are all ticked off … All safe, it seems.

'What about Richard?' He hasn't been working there long.

'Don't know.'

Driving back to the rooms we approach Richard's house, praying his truck is there. It isn't, and there are more cars parked there than normal. The realisation hits.

Two years ago he married his Filipina penpal, a young woman who quickly settled into the community of women from her country living on the Coast, many of whom work at a Greymouth supermarket. Recently, she and Richard had their wedding anniversary at the Working Men's Club. The Filipina women had danced and posed for photographs, and, contrary to liberal prejudice, they didn't seem unhappy. I remember discussing this with a Wellington friend, who immediately tensed up. 'I don't feel comfortable,' she had commented primly. It seemed a statement from a privileged person.

We park the ambulance and Mike comes out to tell us that he's been visiting her, but now her friends have come. Mike is close to tears. Larrie kicks a stone. 'Fuck it.'

In a community, events and places are personalised by the stories that surround them. Richard's house had almost burnt down and he'd built a new structure inside the shell of the old. One day he'd taken down the charred shell and there, like one of those Russian dolls, stood another, smaller, perfect little cottage with exquisite joinery. He liked comic novels – extraordinary works, really: half pornographic, half satirical. I'd given him a copy of Jared Diamond's *Collapse*, a book about the decline of civilisations, and he'd enthused over it.

He'd only been down the mine for a couple of months and when I last spoke to him he said he wasn't enjoying it. Too much the craftsman, too much the loner. 'I never know what I'm supposed to be doing,' he had complained. Hard to imagine him now, huddled, concussed in a corner. Or a charred remnant.

Day Two

It is a grey, drizzly day and cloud coats the surrounding hills. The helicopters buzz to and from the mine but there is no real news. Gas sampling is taking place, that's all we are told. The rescue team is still not going in.

My daughter arrives and we go for our Saturday walk down to the creek. The father of one of her students is among those trapped. My daughter's partner, Darcy, works in Spring Creek mine and last night they'd had a succession of worried phone calls from family and friends. 'It's all a bit close to home,' she says.

I've got a play due to open later in the week and I wonder whether we should cancel. 'People might be preoccupied,' she says. A laconic way of putting it.

That night they come to dinner and we watch the news. Still nothing is happening at Pike. Darcy can't work out why the rescue team hasn't gone in and is suspicious that a cop is in charge. 'What's he know about it?' The view of old-timers is that because the gases are burnt up in the explosion you go in straight away, do what you can, then get out and seal the mine.

John Key looks uncomfortable, as if he's so used to smiling he finds it difficult to keep his face appropriately grim. He reminds me a little of Rosencrantz and Guildenstern, the courtiers in *Hamlet*.

It's a time of waiting, but as we eat there is also a desire for normality. Darcy talks about an ex-skinhead he works with who is covered in tats: Hitler, swastika, and in the middle of it all, Bugs Bunny. The blokes have him on. 'What's Bugs Bunny doing there?' 'It's the first one I got done,' the ex-skinhead tells them.

But after the laughter, thoughts of the disaster return. The mine management is feeding the relatives a hopeful image of the men huddled around a pipe feeding them fresh air – a sort of fairytale. There seems a public-relations quality to the news briefings (and later I will learn that PR people were immediately called in to manage the situation).

We go down to the Working Men's Club for a bit of company. Here, life's going on: the pool table is busy, the CD player turned up. Tony comes over and thanks me for taking him to the hospital in the ambulance a couple of weeks ago. He's okay now – he'd caught pneumonia. Tina is going on about 1080 poison. Pam's come up from Milton because someone's relationship is in trouble and she's here to support her. Normality.

The Spring Creek delegate arrives.

'Why aren't the rescue team in there?' I ask him.

'I'll tell you, comrade,' Trevor says. 'The gas readings are going up, not down. They're frightened of another explosion.'

'Not good.'

'No, not good. It's a big one.'

'There've been rumours it was an unsafe mine ...'

'I know.'

I walk home gloomily. The lights are on in Richard's house. His wife is home. In bed my thoughts turn to Milt, another of those below. I'd got to know him and his family while doing a video on the school closures a few years back. He'd brought a wind-up mallard duck along to the protest march. In relation to the Coast, Labour did some dumb things while in office, Helen Clark's comment about Coasters being 'feral' perhaps being the worst. Closing the schools was a close second.

Day Three

Nothing's changed: still no rescue attempt. I write up the experience so far, then turn to the question of the play. The problem down here for an artist is that most people work with the realities of the physical world. There are not as many people divorced from it – in offices etc, performing intellectual work – as there are in the city, so the imaginative act is apt to seem a mere daydream. In the city, tunnelling through the earth can easily exist as a symbol. Here, it is an occupation.

One reality: Pike River Mining Company is publicly listed. Its main shareholders are New Zealand Oil and Gas (with links to an Australian company) and the Bank of New Zealand (owned by the Australians), but there's also a substantial Indian shareholding interest, plus some Mum and Dad investors. Money so far spent on development? Close to $250 million. Original estimate: $25 million. Who was daydreaming?

I go and open the museum. The village is quiet, but suddenly a bus pulls up and some Dutch tourists alight, existing in that strange time-capsule of the tour party: self-absorbed, cameras at the ready. One woman examines the sculpture that fronts the complex, and the Māori carving particularly captures her attention. I explain that it represents Ngā Hau a Wha, people brought by the four winds to work in the mines. She takes a photo, then they are off to the next place.

I've been told there's a wheel from the overhead that used to carry the coal from Blackball to Ngahere lying in the bush over the road, so I take a saw and pruning shears and begin to hunt through the gorse and blackberry. Just as I'm about to give up, I spy an old washing machine and a pile of other rubbish. I cut my way to it and a metre away is the rim of the wheel. I clear the gorse and it is of admirable size and structure. Mounted near the museum it will become a memorial to those killed at work, a kaupapa which, right now, is overly resonant.

Day Four

The tone has changed. What has perhaps been obvious all along, from the moment the ambulance crews were stood down – that these men are dead – is now being gently implied. Are these things planned? If so, the images of family grieving become images of people's emotions manipulated by experts. The politicians begin to talk of an inquiry.

This has become a site of excess and scarcity. There is an excess of technology, knowledge and skill, and a scarcity of opportunity, or an unwillingness to use it. The earth smoulders and all that technology is useless. Greenies say we should leave the captured CO_2 in the ground. Are they right? This disaster certainly questions the idea of mines in national parks.

I finish mowing the lawns, the task I was doing four days ago, then decide to continue on to Richard's section, where the grass has grown long. I get his front yard tidied before my mower overheats. Colin drives up and tells me Richard was working down the mine to save up enough money to build a house for his wife's parents in the Philippines. It becomes, like so many stories, a global one.

The radio tells me that the bore-hole down to the mine will be finished tonight and that robots stand poised, but the message between the lines is clear: the mine's atmosphere is poisonous and the men are dead. A father complains about there having been no rescue attempt. 'They went down Strongman straight away. That was the best time.'

I think back to my interview with the Strongman rescuers. It was hellishly hot, but they extracted all the bodies bar two, before it became too dangerous. They had operated from the simple ethic of solidarity: They're our mates down there and we have to get them out. Maybe nowadays there's too much risk management, too many protocols. And in contrast the ludicrously simple is used: they're tying a rag to the robot to see if there's any wind current in the tunnel.

We rehearse the play and invite Mike and his kids to watch. In the tension of playing to an audience I am reminded of St Paul's maxim: Wherever two people are gathered …

The helicopters continue to fly overhead.

The policeman in charge talks, finally, about the possibility that some of the men are dead.

Day Five

There is a crowd of cars at Richard's place – his wife, who had been staying with friends, has come back. As we hug I notice she seems to have become even smaller, her face all tears and lips, the ego crumpled, overwhelmed. Richard's mother introduces herself, and then they have to go back to another Pike family meeting. 'Where they'll tell us the same old things,' she says cynically.

People are starting to get pissed off. It seems the robot managed 500 metres then broke down because of water dripping onto it. 'Why the hell didn't they put plastic over it?' fumes the mayor. 'Don't they know mines are wet places?'

Still, more toys are coming – from Australia, from the US. But even NASA won't solve this one.

On the news at six there is CCTV footage of the mine entrance at the time of the explosion. For the first time we see the forces that were at work – for a sustained period of time. And this was two kilometres away, with half the force of the explosion having vented through the ventilation shaft. Apart from the two who got out, no one could have survived that. The inevitable question is asked: 'Why didn't you show us this before?' Presumably the PR company told them it would be unwise.

In the old days – before kids were stopped from climbing trees, before risk assessment forms were required in order for a class of school children to walk around the block, before a spot of rust on a car bonnet made the vehicle 'unsafe', before cycling to the shop without a helmet became illegal – maybe they would have gone straight in. Maybe, after they'd had a look inside, and taking into account the distance they would have been required to walk (2.5km) and the risk of another explosion, they would have said, 'Look, if they're not out by now, they're dead. We need to seal the mine so we can get in there in a few days' time and get the bodies out.'

Maybe then the families could have gone home and started the grieving process. Instead, there's been this drip-feeding of hope and despair, hope and despair.

The Engineering, Printing and Manufacturing Union calls for the return of a mine inspectorate. I remember the Strongman people wanting the same thing. One of the rescue team had left mining and bought a takeaway bar. 'The health and safety manual for the takeaway bar is as thick as a bloody encyclopaedia,' he'd reported, 'whereas the manual for a mine is as thin as a kids' cookbook. It's bloody ridiculous.'

The evening ends with a documentary on Rapanui, Easter Island, one of the subjects of the book on collapsing civilisations I had lent Richard.

To sleep, perchance to dream. As I fall asleep, Hamlet's monologue flicks through my mind.

Day Six

My partner Caroline's car fails a warrant because of uneven rear braking so I drive down to Darcy's to use his trolley jack, take off the wheels and brake drums and clean out the gunk.

He's been back down the mine at Spring Creek and I ask him how it feels. 'The thought's there,' he says. I tell him these disasters seem to occur at 50-year intervals so he should be okay.

I clean the rehearsal space before going home, where I turn on the radio and there it is: a second explosion, even bigger than the first. The mine has probably collapsed and the coal seam could be on fire. Convenient, in a way. There will be little forensic evidence left. Finally, what has been obvious during the past days – that the 29 men are dead – is acknowledged.

On the news at six, one of the fathers, a lean, unforgiving man, analyses the week. 'Should've gone in. The rest of it's been a PR exercise,' he says. But the Pike River CEO, Peter Whittall, a rotund uncle of a man, who has continued to face up to the cameras and has thus gained everyone's respect, continues 'the exercise' in the best possible way. Two kinds of people, really. Now the opera of solace begins – from church and state. We eat a sombre meal, then I remember there's a meeting and a working bee at the swimming pool. 'Surely they will have cancelled it?' says Caroline.

But no, everyone's there, the kids catching tadpoles and small frogs in the muddy water that has accumulated at the deep end of this pool dug out by the miners while on strike in 1908. We discuss the problems of maintaining a community pool on a voluntary basis, given the ever-increasing volume of health and safety requirements, the incessant need to check water quality, the price of chemicals, the requirement to have a trained lifeguard in attendance, the exorbitant cost of a new pool liner … on it goes. Tens of thousands of dollars are involved. Without the pool the kids would go down to the river – a lot more risky. But local solutions will not be tolerated. The world must be safe. Yeah, right.

After the meeting there is a cacophony of lawnmowers and weedeaters. Richard's house silently watches this frantic activity, which could be seen as an avoidance of grief. Caroline shakes her head.

'What's the problem?' I ask.

'Things should stop for a while.'

Afterwards people go to a variety of wakes. We gather some flowers and take them around to the museum. Mike and his family join us and we sing, 'Kia whakarongo ake, ki te tangi …' Their daughter cries. On the way home a little boy on a bike proudly shows us the graze he suffered when he fell off. 'It almost bled,' I say, and he vigorously nods.

Day Seven

We were to have had a private performance tonight, but cast members have emailed saying it is inappropriate. So, a series of phone calls before I go into Greymouth for the first time since the explosion. The tourist train has arrived and the hustle of buses and rental cars is normal, but I don't know what to say to the bank teller or to the supermarket checkout operator when she tells me to have a nice day.

The union office displays emails of support from around the

world. The council lawn is scattered with satellite dishes and tents, and reporters are filmed as they give their update. Tony wanders along. 'About time those bastards pissed off,' he says after we hongi.

I head up to the school where my daughter teaches. I pause at the principal's office and we talk over the situation. She tells me that being in a school at a time like this is in many ways a good thing – a normalising process – for the children demand the same level of input. They don't care.

'Like the birds,' I say.

'Exactly.' She pities the surviving miners, many of them from overseas, who may well now be out of work.

The paper's front page features photos of the 29 dead. A trust fund is being set up for the families. Darcy is off fishing and my daughter comes to dinner. I ask her how he's coping.

'He's fine,' she reports. 'He just needed to go back to work.'

At the end-of-year dinner his foreman had told her Darcy would get to be shift leader, and then he'd be able to work anywhere in the world.

'It means he's not just a labourer all his life,' she says. Some of their Wellington friends are a bit snooty about the Coast, but they don't understand. 'Since coming down here, I realise mining's a culture,' she says. As for the danger, when Darcy worked on construction sites in Wellington there were at least two people killed a year. Add those deaths up …

Afterwards we go down to the Hilton where the union officials are staying. They sit at dinner with the secretary's phone going at regular intervals: BBC, Radio Ireland, New York … Yet I can't help feeling disenchanted. Courtier stuff really. Rosencrantz and Guildenstern again, with CNN for King Claudius. Is this the 1984 Orwell worried over, created not by some dictator but simply by everyone playing their part? Hamlet has crept in again. There's something rotten … Mark me …

At that point I stopped the diary.

The writing of this book began then at this personal level. But of course after a week there were already other responses. The local paper, as well as reporting what was happening (or not happening), published pages of poems and letters of condolence from locals and from afar. As a nation, we continue to be emotionally energised by disaster, with the military catastrophe of the Gallipoli campaign the primal ritual of nationhood. The 'objective' inquiries were about to begin (Department of Labour, Police) and a royal commission was being set up.

Throughout the week Pike had been compared to another recent event – the Chilean goldminers who, after being trapped underground for 69 days, were miraculously rescued. Performances here were compared to performances there. But, unlike Chile, as a drama Pike was curiously static and wordy, for nothing much, after the initial explosion, actually happened – other than a second explosion. There was no rescue action.

There were four main players in the local drama: the policeman in charge, Superintendent Garry Knowles, who came across as wooden (and whose role was seriously questioned); Pike River CEO Peter Whittall, who, undoubtedly coached by the PR team, played the brave, cuddly (and in need of a cuddle) grandfather; Grey District Mayor Tony Kokshoorn, who provided the suffering local face; and John Key, the Prime Minister, having to play undertaker – an unfamiliar role, for normally his part is that of the laid-back, unfazed Kiwi bloke. The family members were a chorus of grieving peasants – weeping, hugging and occasionally angry. The dead miners themselves were for days nameless, and then they featured on the front covers of papers as instant heroes.

After the Brunner and Strongman disasters the dead were buried in mass graves, with a whole community in attendance. On the day of the Strongman burials the rain came down in buckets as the cortege drove through the packed streets. But funerals for those killed in Pike River could not be immediately held, for there were no bodies and no coroner's hearing. There was no physical presence over which families could mourn. To fill the gap, the government decided on a memorial service, which played on national television.

The function of a memorial service is 'to preserve in memory' and 'to celebrate in speech and writing'. But a disaster is preserved to what end? There were attempts to celebrate the dead men as heroes: brave underground miners facing danger every day, but the truth is they were normal blokes doing a day's work, and this should never have happened.

On the day of the service, staged by the government's event management team at the Omoto Racecourse, most of Greymouth turned out, joined by Coasters who came home for the day from Christchurch. There was a strange configuration: the dignitaries on one side of the racetrack in a temporary grandstand, the ordinary people on the other side of the fence. The families sat in the normal grandstand, facing the dignitaries, the young women dressed in their best, faces well made up, the men looking uncomfortable in shiny suits. The union was not invited to speak.

The intent, often Irish faces of the locals basked in the sun, listening but strangely detached. As the service unfolded, speakers from church, state and corporation appeared on large screens and were relayed nationally and internationally, to provide images for the networks: of the nation grieving, of the dignitaries doing their job, of Greymouth watching ... French philosopher Jean Baudrillard compares the electronic media to a virus, which invades the body and attaches itself to healthy cells.[7] In this case the media attached itself to what should have been a community ritual and turned it into an electronic 'otherness', which multiplied ad infinitum.

But resistance was beginning to form to this distortion. Anger was already being expressed in private at the family meetings. If organised, such anger can build a coalition of the recalcitrant.

But the recalcitrant were not organised at the political level.

Once upon a time on the Coast, they were. Investigating this change becomes, then, the first demand that this event creates.

CHAPTER TWO

Hard Labour

Workers of the world

Coal was created in the Carbinoferous period, 200–300 million years ago, when giant fern-like trees fell and were covered by water, which stopped them decaying. They were subsequently heated and compressed. These trees had absorbed CO^2 (carbon dioxide) from the CO^2-rich atmosphere and pumped out oxygen in return. With less CO^2 and more oxygen in the atmosphere the planet cooled, the ocean currents began circulating, oxygenating the water, weather patterns became more stable and the biosystem as we know it was established.

As then Green Party leader Jeanette Fitzsimons pointed out in a debate with local miners that was the centrepiece of the 2005 Blackball Mayday celebrations, these seams of coal are stored carbon dioxide (CO^2). As is oil. And when we burn the coal and the oil the stored CO^2 is returned to the atmosphere. If you return the CO^2 to the atmosphere, as we have been doing for the past 150 years, the planet will go back to what it was. But with the stark difference that the act of releasing this stored CO^2 has meanwhile radically changed society. Coal fuelled the industrial revolution, that radical change in production methods that led to such rapid change that we now seem to be standing, disoriented, on the brink of catastrophe. Barbara Freese writes in her book on the human history of coal:

The lives of factory workers in Manchester, and in the other new industrial cities rising up around Britain, were shaped by the burning of coal just as the coal miners' lives were shaped by the digging of it. Coal made the iron that built the machines the workers operated as well as the factories they worked in and then it provided the power that made the machines and factories run. Coal gas provided the lights the workers toiled under, letting their workday start before dawn and end after dusk.[8]

For coal enabled the steam engine, which in turn enabled deeper underground mining, as the engine could pump out the water and circulate the air. The steam engine created the modern factory and, in turn, the modern city, and when it became mobile it revolutionised transport. Coal could be turned into coke, essential to the smelting of iron ore and steel. Coal also fuelled the wood and coal range, which was at the centre of the domestic house, providing heat, cooking and hot water.

Finally, coal created the working class: people who did not own the means of production and who had only their labour to sell. Freese describes the process:

The displaced workers from the home-based workshops, along with farmers driven off their land by the agricultural reforms of the time, were then available to staff the urban mills. They were not forming the first industrial community in Britain; the coal miners of Newcastle, working for wages in large, high capital mines, had beaten them to it by a couple of centuries. Still, the factory workers of Manchester and the other booming industrial cities were forming something new to the world: a large class of people whose lives were shaped, and in many ways reduced, by machines.[9]

Little wonder, then, that on the other side of the world Thomas Brunner showed keen interest when local Māori pointed out a coal seam on the banks of the Grey River, 20km from the river mouth. But it took some years before the seam was exploited.

Mines, if of any size, are capital-intensive operations. For as well as developing the mine itself, a complex infrastructure has to be built to transport the coal to its destination. In the case of the Blackball mine, for example, first established in the 1890s, this initially involved an overhead aerial carrying coal buckets across the river to the railway line at Ngahere. In the case of Denniston, the famous incline had to be constructed and maintained.[10]

The owners of these early mines performed the complex dance of colonial capitalism. The Blackball mine was initially developed by local capital with input from Dunedin and Christchurch. But because of high development costs and a local market undermined by Australian imports it proved unsustainable until bought by an English shipping company that required fuel for the return journey of its ships to Britain.

And of course there was the cost of housing the workers in locations remote from the established towns. Accordingly, the Blackball Shipping Company bought up the land on the plateau near the mine and leased sections to workers to build houses. The company also constructed a mine manager's villa and some single men's huts.

Whenever a ship came into port the company needed a lot of coal quickly, but after the ship had gone, with only the local market to supply, demand dropped right back. Accordingly, periods of high production alternated with periods of low production, and an on-call, casual workforce was, from the owners' point of view, the ideal.

But on-call, casual work is unsatisfactory for the worker, as it means an irregular and uncertain income. In a remote location other work is not available. And the workers knew that their product was, at times of peak demand, vital to the company. Tensions were, then, endemic to the operation. This pattern repeated itself at most New Zealand coalmines.

By the late 19th century the new class of people created by industrialism – the proletariat – had an understanding of their role in society, and the contradictions of that role. On the one hand they were wage slaves without ownership or control. On the other, they were free to negotiate the cost and the conditions of their labour. If negotiations failed, they could go on strike and deny the owner their labour, in which case their loss of wages, and their family's immediate poverty, were balanced against the loss of income to the capitalist.

They naturally became aware of their collective power. Marx and

Engels' battle cry – 'The proletarians have nothing to lose but their chains. They have a world to win. Working men of all countries unite!' – had been sounded.[11] The union movement in Britain had matured in terms of organisation and begun to be a player on the political scene. The working class had begun to organise its experience, to educate itself, to create its own culture and to express this knowledge and this culture in tract, song and banner.[12]

On the memorial to the 1908 Blackball strike are the words of a verse of one of these songs:

> They have taken untold millions
> That they never toiled to earn
> Yet without our brain and muscle
> Not a single wheel can turn.
> We can break their haughty power
> Gain our freedom when we learn
> That the union makes us strong.[13]

Today the words may appear quaint, yet, if sung outside the office of some speculator in futures or sub-prime mortgages taking home a bonus of millions, they retain the ring of truth.

But there was a contradiction. Working people migrated to New Zealand in order to get on, and getting on meant acquiring a block of land or creating a small business. There was a petit bourgeois, even a gentry aspiration among many of the tradesmen. At the other end of the spectrum there was the phenomenon that historian James Belich calls 'crew culture': men working in gangs – sailors, sealers, shearers, forestry workers – out of contact with the rest of society for lengthy periods, then hitting town for a good time. This was a sub-proletariat without the developing working-class consciousness of the conventional force of workers in factories and mines, or on the wharves and the railways.[14]

In this mix, coalminers formed an elite of manual labourers, and this remains the case, for it is a job that cannot be easily learnt. Miners will talk about listening to the earth, being able to interpret the creaks and groans, of knowing when a fall is likely. The environment is hazardous and claustrophobic and you have to be able to trust your fellow workers. Back then, without modern machinery, it was hard work, there was a large workforce, the bosses were often remote capitalists from England and the product was essential. In the words of the anthem:

> In our hands there is a power
> Greater than their hoarded gold
> Greater than the mighty atom
> Magnified a thousandfold.
> We can bring to birth a new world
> From the ashes of the old
> For our union makes us strong.

A strong union movement had grown up around mining in Britain, and the workers brought the culture of that movement to New Zealand. The coalmines here were worked by immigrants rather than by the locally born. Len Richardson, in his history of coalminers, *Coal, Class and Community*, points out that in New Zealand miners lived in isolated communities with the whole community focused on the mine, so that more general societal influences (gentry aspiration, crew culture etc) did not impact. It is little surprise, then, that they became a vanguard of the working class in this country.[15]

By the end of the 19th century there was a variety of political paradigms present. Free-marketeers believed that market forces (with labour being simply another resource) should be allowed to control society. Government's role should be limited to foreign relations, with the focus on assisting local capitalists to access resources and markets, and at home to combating criminality or combinations that distorted the market (such as unions).

Opposing this ideology, one faction of communists, following Marx, were of the belief that the workers, led by the Communist Party, should capture the state (whose function was to protect the power of the ruling class) through a revolution, and the state should then take over the means of production and administer the economy without recourse to the market, but according to the maxim 'From each according to his ability, to each according to his need'. After a transition period of dictatorship by the working class, during which relations of mutuality would be established, the state would wither away.

A faction of libertarian socialists (anarcho-syndicalists), following Bakunin and others, believed that the state and the market were equally suspect, and instead society should be organised locally, from the bottom up, with relations of mutuality established from the outset. Unions were a good example of the grassroots organisation, and a coalition (syndicate) of these unions could confront the coalition of capital.

Finally, social democrats, the Fabians being the first articulators, accepted the market, but believed that the state had a significant role to play by tempering market forces in the interests of rational economic development and in order to protect the vulnerable. State ownership of essential infrastructure was required in order to do this. In this compromise view the state, unions (representing the working class) and business should negotiate for a socially just society. This tripartite model, which came to prevail in New Zealand, is criticised on the one hand by the free-marketeers as leading to market distortions, and on the other, by the syndicalists and communists, as being a mystification, in that the contradictions of capitalism can never be resolved.

The pendulum swings, country by country, circumstance by circumstance. Generally, from a broad working-class point of view, the historic task has been to at least establish the framework and the expectation of social democracy as the norm in the minds of the majority of the voters. In no country has this been an easy task, and the coalminers played a central role in the struggle to do so in Aotearoa.

A decade of radicalism

Coalmining was established on the Coast by the 1880s and a workers' leader quickly emerged. Based in Denniston, Frederick Lomas, a Welsh Methodist, in Richardson's words 'waged a civil war on two fronts. On the one hand he challenged colonial employers to accept unions as an integral part of the workplace. On the other hand, he warned miners against the dangers of the bar-rail [spending their free time in the pub].'[16]

When the Australian watersiders, on strike in 1890 in order to force the employers to recognise their union, called on their New Zealand comrades to support them, the Kiwis put a ban on loading and unloading Australian ships. Local employers brought in scab labour and the government provided soldiers to protect them. The miners and seamen joined the wharfies and the 1890 maritime strike unfolded. After three months of bitter struggle the unions caved in.

A commission to investigate the strike was scathing of the miners, who had played a prominent role. Colliers, they reported, 'lacked the pride of colonials, had lower ideas of life, inferior morals and stronger prejudices than were found amongst the general population'. (Helen Clark was to echo this judgement with her 'feral' epithet for Coasters.) The collectivist ethos of unionism was condemned as a grasping attempt by a handful of migrants to carve out for themselves a privileged position in the colony, or as the exercise of 'despotic power' by a 'few headstrong individuals'.[17]

Despite the setback of the 1890 strike the political environment became more favourable to union formation. With the 1891 election of a Liberal government (with West Coaster Richard Seddon in its ranks), the time was ripe for political representation for working people. Accordingly, women were given the vote in 1893, and in 1894 the Industrial Conciliation and Arbitration Act was passed, making unions legal bodies with which employers had to negotiate, and setting up an Arbitration Court to hear and adjudicate disputes. This was progressive legislation and it was hoped that the IC&A Act would end strikes. People came from all over the world to see this 'grassroots socialism' in action.

Already, as part of union-building, the major content of the mining unions' demands had emerged, and to this day the content has not significantly changed.

- A national agreement rather than local agreements.
- Better wages, with an hourly rate rather than contract or piece-work systems.
- Consistent hours, rather than spasmodic casual, on-call work. To

this end unions tried to put in place work-sharing systems when there was limited work because of low demand, and to limit output to stop the employers stockpiling.

• There were sufficient accidents and disasters (Kaitangata, 1879; Brunner, 1896) for health and safety to be a priority. Unions sought:

    i.   improved sanitation underground;

    ii.   a limited length to shifts (8 hours), to prevent exhaustion;

    iii.   no dogwatch (night shift) because of its impact on individual and family life;

    iv.   inspection of pits by workers' representatives who had authority ('check inspectors');

    v.   mining experience to be recognised as a necessity (this required a move away from stop-start production and the employment of individuals 'off the street').

• Improved social and living conditions. In isolated mining communities the living conditions were often atrocious, with single men and families living in temporary one-room shacks with few amenities. There was a call for pensions for miners once they reached the age of 60, and for miner representation on public bodies relevant to the industry.

How to gain these demands was the task. Common sense might indicate that state ownership of mines would resolve many of these issues, and indeed, early in the century, the state set up the Runanga coalmine and established the township. This, perhaps inevitably, started workers down the social democratic path to the 1935 election of a Labour government.

But in the interim, and in a decade that produced, in Richardson's view, 'an astonishingly creative burst of activity', the libertarian socialist framework was to the fore. This resulted in 'a national miners federation and a national federation of labour, a national labour newspaper, a prolonged campaign for reform of working and living conditions, the election of a first coalminer politician, and an attempt to re-organise the labour movement along syndicalist lines'.[18]

It is hard to get into the head-space of the radical worker back then. Postmodernism has eradicated the over-arching narrative of social redemption in which they were immersed. And in between this period and the postmodern were the welfare-state decades of relative comfort.

Auckland art-in-working-life artist Phill Rooke designed the sculpture for the 1908 strike memorial in Blackball, erected in 2010. The red flag symbolises that socialism was at the heart of the struggle; that is, the belief in the common ownership of the means of production, distribution and exchange. Red because blood had been shed for the cause. The five points of the star can be the five fingers of a worker's hand, or the five continents, or the five groups that will create socialism: youth, the military, workers, peasants and the intelligentsia. The triangle at the top of the sculpture points to hope for a better future (in Fidel Castro's motto: a better world is possible). And then there are symbols of industrialism: ropes, shackles, bolts and timber – materials with which the worker works. Local carver Tony Manuel (Ngāti Porou) added a Māori 'eye' to the sculpture. He used the pattern found on food-storage houses, which also symbolised the fact that the workers came from the four corners of the globe, driven by the four winds.

A play I wrote about the 1908 strike, based largely on Eric Beardsley's novel *Blackball '08*,[19] begins with a miner at the coal face reciting from the *Communist Manifesto*: 'Society is more and more splitting into two great hostile camps, into two great classes directly facing each other: Bourgeoisie and Proletariat.'

A few scenes later Bob Semple addresses an audience of miners:

It's perfectly obvious that the system, as it is, is set up to benefit the parasites: the bosses and their wives in silks and furs, their lackeys, the lawyers, the managers, the politicians as well, living a life of luxury on the backs of the workers. But we have the strength of our solidarity. If we join together, union and union into a unity of unions, a federation at the national level, even the international level, we can confront capital and smash its structures and run the world for the good of all.[20]

These men, working and living in difficult conditions, isolated, with the migrant urge to improve their lot, open to rhetoric and oratory, dreamed this potent dream, tempered by the physical reality of working at the coal face. And there were the necessary activists, men driven to change the world. Pat Hickey (New Zealand born of Irish parents) and Australians Bob Semple and Paddy Webb were influenced by the Industrial Workers of the World movement ('Wobblies'), which preached the above mission rather than a gentler social democratic reformism. The movement was born in the US, where worker–boss negotiations often involved armed thugs hired by the boss gunning down recalcitrant workers. It was a movement where workers had died in the class struggle.

> The people's flag is deepest red
> It shrouded oft our martyred dead
> And 'ere the corpse was stiff and cold
> Its blood had stained every fold.[21]

The sheer differences – in housing, in clothing, in education, in expectation – between the classes gave birth to these narratives of revolt in these 'primitive, remote and almost inaccessible camps'.[22] These camps were not inaccessible to ideas, or to the occasional visit by international speakers on the socialist circuit. And there was always an element of preaching and of church, with songbooks and tracts and a religious fervour present.

The arbitration system worked well for a short period, but by the early 20th century the judges were perceived as being biased in the employers' favour and the system something of a straitjacket in the task of confronting capital as a united body of workers. Hickey, Semple and Webb targeted Blackball as a volatile workplace because of stop–start production, because of arguments over shifts, because of living conditions and because of the infamous 15-minute 'crib-time' (lunchtime).

Early in 1908, galvanised by a provocative manager, the workers struck over their crib-time, thumbed their noses at the Arbitration Court and stayed out for three months, supported by New Zealand and Australian workers. Their eventual victory was due as much to good luck as fortitude, but a victory it was, and well publicised in the national media. Richardson writes:

There was no denying the enthusiasm which the victory engendered throughout the West Coast coalfields. The excitement of the struggle, the defiant displays of solidarity and the ridiculing of the Arbitration Court, raised a variety of expectations. The more extravagant were moved to urge a revolutionary assault upon the capitalist system.[23]

There had also been developments elsewhere. In the three years preceding the Blackball strike, Runanga had been established as a state-owned mine, with Bob Semple becoming president of the union. A co-operative society was formed, which ran a store and built the iconic Miners' Hall, on the front of which a slogan called for 'World's Wealth for World's Workers'. Further north, the Westport mines of Denniston and Millerton were even more unpleasant and bred their own volatility.

After the 1908 strike the miners' unions formed a national body, the New Zealand Federation of Miners, which stated in the preamble to its constitution:

> We hold that all men are created to be free, and should have equal access and opportunity to the enjoyment of all benefits to be derived from their exertions in dealing with the natural resources of the earth, and that free access and equal opportunity thereto are absolutely necessary to man's existence and the upward progress of the human race …[24]

A year later they changed their name to the New Zealand Federation of Labour (NZFL), soon to be popularly known as the Red Feds. Watersiders, general labourers, shearers and other mainly labour-type unions soon affiliated. The federation took over the labour newspaper, the *Maoriland Worker* (circulation 10,000), and encouraged aggressive action in industrial disputes.

It was a period during which a revolutionary fervour was felt in New Zealand, when the struggle for social justice moved outside the political mainstream, and the model of direct action was widely adopted. As people found during the 1981 Springbok tour protests, such a model of action is liberating: forget collecting signatures for petitions, lobbying MPs, writing letters to the paper, attending select committee hearings – take to the streets instead. Or go on strike. And don't be afraid of the law. The world doesn't end if you get arrested.

After a series of successful industrial skirmishes the NZFL confronted as well the growing climate of militarism. In 1909 compulsory military training was introduced for boys between 12 and 21. In 1911 this was extended to adult males. The socialists proudly proclaimed that they recognised no enemy other than the exploiters of labour, and in February 1912, Richardson reports, the miners celebrated 80 defaulters in Runanga alone. In Millerton not one boy presented himself for drill. Instead they assembled outside the drill shed and sang 'The Red Flag'.[25]

The employers and the government were not amused. During the six-month-long Waihi strike of 1912, caused by the formation of a company-inspired breakaway union, and which led to the death of striker Frederick Evans, the presence of armed scabs and the heavy police approach were warnings of things to come. In 1913 the NZFL expanded to become the United Federation of Labour. But the 1913 waterfront dispute, which began with a miners' strike in Huntly, can be seen as having been deliberately engineered by the employers, backed by a government determined to strike at the heart of the militant union movement.[26]

When farmers were called in from the country districts and sworn in as special constables, violent street battles erupted. Dozens of people were injured and guns waved around. Sir Joseph Ward, speaking in parliament, described it as 'a system of Mexican revolt and civil war, a system of our own kith and kin from the country being brought down against our own kith and kin in the town to use force for the settlement of an industrial dispute'.[27]

The miners had struck in solidarity, and civic leaders on the Coast complained that intimidation by miners had reached intolerable levels. The Greymouth Inspector of Police stated:

> The men employed in the mines are principally socialists and anyone
> who differs from them gets a warm time until they are forced to
> leave or join their ranks. I fear if something is not done by the

Government to remedy the existing state of things serious trouble
will yet arise.[28]

Edward Hunter, one of the miners' leaders, responded to this
threat at a rally in Wellington:

> There is a Mayor in Westport but he has been set aside, and every-
> thing is controlled by the strikers. They can bring the 'specials' round
> to the Coast, in fact, we give them a special invitation, and I swear
> this, in the name of the party most concerned, that for every one
> 'special' they care to put down on the Coast, up to one thousand, we
> can put down one beside him, just as good a man, and if this is going
> to be a contest as to who is going to control, then we are prepared to
> make it a contest.[29]

Heady stuff. But after six weeks the strike ended in defeat for the
UFL. Manned by scabs, the wharves in Auckland and Wellington
reopened, seamen broke ranks and returned to work, and the
federation called off the strike on 20 December, with the miners
returning to work nine days later.

This revolutionary phase of the New Zealand workers' movement was perhaps inevitably doomed to failure for there were
insufficient numbers of an urban proletariat. The tradesmen had a
tradition of conservative unionism and were socially mobile, and, as
it turned out, the rural sector, dependent on exporting, was willing
to take on recalcitrant urban workers.

With World War I, patriotism bloomed, and there was another
mine disaster.[30] But the socialists continued to challenge, portraying
the war as 'a ruse of the capitalist class to set the workers of this
country and the workers of other countries at each others' throats'.[31]
The anti-war movement reached out into the community, with
women significantly joining the campaigns.

As well, there had been activity in the political party sector
during this period. A Socialist Party had been formed in 1901, after
which factions had formed, merged and split again, until a unity
conference established the New Zealand Labour Party in 1916.

When conscription was introduced in that same year the
government used it as a means of locking away leaders of both

the miners' union and the new party. Peter Fraser was convicted of sedition and jailed for 12 months. Bob Semple, Tim Armstrong, Jim O'Brien and Paddy Webb also went to prison, jailed without jury trials. Webb had been elected to parliament by the Grey District in 1913. When he was balloted in 1917 he refused to serve, resigned, then promptly won the by-election. But he was tried by court martial, given two years' hard labour and deprived of his civil rights for a decade. Harry Holland filled his parliamentary seat.

The anti-conscriptors were supported by rank-and-file miners with a strike against the Military Service Act in 1916, a go-slow in 1917, followed by a further strike when their leaders were arrested. Richardson writes:

> The savagery of the government's actions served to intensify the miners' sense of alienation. The arrests and the subsequent release of their leaders from prison provided occasions for festivals of defiance, 'monster demonstrations', 'grand receptions', 'banquets' and 'balls'; at which heroes could be feted, villains pilloried, injustices proclaimed and emotional expression given to the myriad grievances which together made up the collective sense of oppression.[32]

Perhaps we should consider the resistance of these men and their families as the first moment of national maturity, rather than the deaths of thousands of mystified young men trying to dig trenches with their fingernails after being thrown into a badly planned battle thousands of miles from home.

Labour and the red flag

In the Westminster system of government articulate class warfare, which had now been present in New Zealand for two decades, is wisely frowned upon, and at the end of the war a further inquiry was set up, this time a Board of Trade commission of inquiry into the coalmining environment.

Richardson reports that the grim reality of mining townships, with people living in overcrowded makeshift shacks with a lack of sanitation, came as a shock to the commission members. They suggested that if the physical conditions in which the miners and their families lived were improved – by providing creches, art and music classes, cinemas, bath-houses and swimming baths – the behaviour of the miners would become less 'anti-social'. As well, they indicated support for some form of nationalisation. A dominion coal board was suggested, in order to promote co-operation between workers, employers and the community generally, with the aim of there being a more humane form of business organisation. Unless this happened, commissioners warned, there could well occur a 'cataclysm', desired by none but a few revolutionary fanatics and utopian dreamers. Events in post-revolutionary Russia were obviously on their minds.

With the new Labour Party providing a parliamentary option, and the Miners' Federation and what was left of the Labour Alliance (the looser national union organisation that the United Federation of Labour had become) having ties to the party, the struggle in New Zealand shifted ground ideologically and practically. Rather than the union movement seeking to overthrow capitalism, it could become an ally of a parliamentary party, which, by winning an election, would run a worker-friendly government. But this involved the inevitable compromises required to win broad electoral support. Despite retaining socialist rhetoric, and indeed calling for state ownership of some of the means of production, distribution and exchange, the Labour Party was a reformist party. It did not seek to overthrow capitalism. Unions, rather than being revolutionary organisations, would negotiate for the workers within the capitalist structure.

The revolutionary struggle in this next period, then, was taken over by small Marxist groups working within unions with the aim of trying to persuade the membership to restore a revolutionary agenda. The programme of these groups was more Leninist than syndicalist; the Communist Party saw itself as a vanguard leading the way to a revolution in which an aroused proletariat would seize power. This historical process was 'inevitable', with capitalism constantly producing crises that must be exploited. Reformism, as embodied by the Labour Party and collaborating unions, could produce small improvements for the working class, but was doomed to failure, for capitalism cannot be tamed. The communists were generally articulate, dogged and hard working, and so could have a considerable influence within unions.

Bill Balderstone and his wife Annie migrated from the South Yorkshire pits to Blackball via Canada, where Bill came under the influence of a leading Canadian socialist. Joined by Scotsman Angus McLagan, the couple became leading figures in the New Zealand communist movement. The West Coast Communist Federation was set up and urged the establishment of district councils among the mining unions – councils that would have full autonomy and set policy for the national federation. It was Sovietism, West Coast style.

Despite demand for coal remaining low the West Coast miners went on strike in 1921 against wage reductions and again were out for three months. The dispute was handled skilfully by the union, with miners in other areas staying at work and contributing to the strike fund. As a result the Coasters won a wage increase of 15 per cent, proving that direct action remained effective. On the back of this success a new, more radical national organisation, the United Mine Workers of New Zealand, was established. Its preamble read:

> We hold that there is a class struggle in society. And that the struggle is caused by the capitalist class owning the means of production to which the working class must have access in order to live … Between these two classes the struggle must continue until capitalism is abolished. Capitalism can only be abolished by the workers uniting in one class-conscious economic organisation to take and hold the means of production, distribution and exchange by revolutionary industrial and political action.[33]

In 1925, believing the coalfields to be at the centre of the workers' struggle, the New Zealand Communist Party shifted its headquarters to Blackball. McLagan became secretary of both the Communist Party and the United Mine Workers. The number of cadres was small – 30 on the Coast, 15 of them in Blackball – but during this period they had considerable influence.

Annie Balderstone started a socialist Sunday school and the

communists established a children's league called The Young Comrades, which had its own uniform and produced a weekly newspaper they sold at the picture theatre. The Workers' Educational Association was boycotted as reactionary. A town like Blackball was very much union-controlled, with a union-run picture theatre, a union-paid doctor and a union-organised bus timetable. Local shopkeepers needed to be politically sympathetic when the workers were on strike.

With the depression approaching, McLagan gave a remarkably prescient analysis of the crisis and its causes. Richardson reports that he condemned the senseless importation of Australian coal while New Zealand mines lay idle, and presented it as a clear example of capitalism's relentless search for profits and disregard for workers' interests. McLagan considered the fundamental cause of mass joblessness to be capitalism's inexorable drive to increase production, unmatched by a comparable increase in spending power. He recommended an expansionary cure: a shorter working week and day, a raising of the school leaving age and the introduction of a retirement age, along with a pension.[34]

But analysis does not on its own change reality, and coal companies facing hard times wanted to reduce their workforces and cut wages. As well, two new (and in the union's view dangerous) production methods were gaining traction.

Co-operatives, whereby a group of workers owned and worked a small seam in a shared manner, had been around for a time. But often, as original partners moved on or fell out, these evolved into a more traditional, small business, owner–worker model. And now, a new production model called tributism arose. In this a labour-only company leased a mine from the owner and sold the coal produced to the owner at a previously agreed price, or gave the owner a proportion of the sale price.

In union eyes both these models posed a threat to workers' wages and conditions, for they encouraged a speeding up of work rates and thereby potentially unsafe practices. As well, these mines could continue to produce coal during strike situations. But they were attractive propositions to mine owners on the verge of bankruptcy.

According to Richardson, the Blackball Coal Company had been in financial difficulties since the mid-1920s and was in danger of closing. In 1931 it chose instead to dismiss the entire workforce and to then re-open, operating a single shift with reduced wages and conditions. The unions insisted instead on rationing the available work across the whole workforce. When the company rejected their position they went on strike.

The strike lasted a bitter five months before a bombshell struck. Bill Balderstone, the ardent communist, announced that he had formed the Blackball Creek Coal Company, which would mine a portion of the Blackball mine on a tribute basis. Those wanting work should apply. Uproar resulted, and 35 police had to be called in to protect the 'scabs'. It is hard to fathom Balderstone's motives in turning capitalist. Perhaps he'd heard of Stalin's labour camps? Perhaps he had decided to take the libertarian socialist path? Maybe he was foretelling the break-up of the Soviet Union, when party officials turned overnight into businessmen?

Anyway, he was hated in the town forever more. If the Balderstones went to the pictures the rest of the patrons walked out. I heard of Balderstone's great-granddaughter visiting the village decades later and being shunned by an elderly woman. Once a scab always a scab. It was certainly the end of Soviet-style communism in Blackball.

But Balderstone's mine survived, as he took on strays from other coalfields and Australia and Canada. Among the rest of the Blackball miners poverty was rife and they had once again to go fossicking for gold. Eventually gold prospecting was added to the list of relief work schemes.

Toward the end of the Depression Angus McLagan, who had broken with the Communist Party in 1929, initiated a push to restore West Coast wages and conditions. In 1934 he led a protest march of unionists and demanded payment of union rates to all relief workers; the abolition of relief camps; the negotiation of a national agreement for miners; as well as improved safety, including supplying hard hats to all miners.

With the election approaching in 1935 there was a thawing of relations between the radically inclined miners and the reformist Labour Party, with the miners campaigning for Labour's eventual victory, which saw the introduction of the welfare state, the nationalising of the mines, and a system of national awards.

After World War II there was a period of relative stability under state ownership, but also a slow running-down of the coalmines, with the National government elected in 1949 taking on the activist unions in the 1951 waterfront lockout. And then in the 1960s the state closed many mines, as diesel and electricity became the preferred fuels. There was as well an urgent need to adopt new technology and modern mining practices.

But the miners had played a vanguard role in the New Zealand's union movement up to that time. For Richardson:

> In the 70-odd years after 1880 during which the transport-related industries assumed a central role in an export economy, the miners had been one of the frontrunners of industrial unionism. Together with the watersiders and the seamen, they gave coherence and structure to the major periods of 'labour unrest'.

He goes on to summarise their achievements:

- giving shape to the new phenomenon of unionism in the late 19th century;
- being a catalyst for the wave of revolutionary syndicalism in the first decade of the 20th century;
- unsettling the false honeymoon between capital and labour, post WWII;
- putting their power to political purposes in anti-conscription and peace campaigns;
- fighting for safe working conditions and more humane towns;
- advocating a policy of expansion rather than retraction during the depression and insisting that the new Labour government nationalise the mines.[35]

It was a considerable achievement, and one that is seldom officially celebrated.

With the closure of the Blackball mine the town should have

died. The mine, after all, was its sole reason for existing. The houses were worthless and most people moved away. But some of the stubborn stayed, cottages were bought as holiday homes, and the hippies arrived. They could afford a house, dope grew well and Gaia was on your doorstep. The transition had begun. The same applied to many other villages on the Coast.

CHAPTER THREE

Health and Safety

A dirty, dangerous job

Within this political narrative it is necessary to consider the issues of health and safety and the influence of technological change, for they are central to the Pike River event.

Underground mining is dangerous – even more so on the West Coast, which is geologically complex, with changes in strata occurring at short intervals.

If you dig a tunnel, the tunnel can fall in, crushing or at least trapping you. That is the first danger.

The second danger comes from the nature of the material you are digging out. Coal, with its vegetative origin, generates methane, CO_2 and carbon monoxide, among other gases. Carbon monoxide binds itself to red blood cells, denying oxygen the same role. If there is too much CO_2 there is too little oxygen. In either case we effectively suffocate. Methane, when combined in the right proportions with oxygen, is explosive if ignited. This explosion can lift the coal dust that accumulates on the floor and tunnel sides into the air, set this coal dust alight and a rolling ball of fire travels through the tunnels, killing those present. The force of any explosion is of course amplified by the confined space. The methane problem is not confined to the present coal being worked; the gas can build up in old workings and it is necessary to seal these off to prevent seepage. A coal seam catching fire is a further problem, for it is extremely difficult to extinguish.

The third danger comes from inundation by water that has built up in old workings. If these workings are accidentally accessed, flooding occurs.

The fourth danger is the coal face itself exploding through the accumulation of myriad pressures, the explosion shooting out a spray of pellets potentially fatal to anyone in the vicinity.

And then there are the usual accidents that can occur with industrial machinery: workers getting trapped, broken or crushed.

Health and safety in mining is therefore a significant issue.

Tunnel collapse was controlled pre-1970 by leaving pillars of coal and putting up wooden props and beams (sets) to hold up the roof of the tunnels created around the pillars. Experienced miners became expert at reading these props and beams, both visually and aurally, as they indicated the pressures being exerted by the earth above. Now, deep holes are drilled in the roof and tunnel sides and bolts grouted in and tightened, so that the layers of rock and coal are squeezed and tied together.

Preventing explosions has remained a complex task, for light is necessary. In the 19th century the safety lamp was invented, replacing the traditional and highly dangerous open flame. In the safety lamp the flame was protected by a fine gauze that let in oxygen but prevented the flame from igniting the methane (fire damp). The flame of the safety lamp would change colour if the methane level was high. The lamp could also be used to detect CO_2, which is heavier than air. If the flame burnt lower or went out when the lamp was placed on the ground, then CO_2 (black damp) was present. Carbon monoxide was detected by a canary in a cage. If the canary keeled over, it was a sign of the gas. Early in the 20th century the SPCA campaigned for a little bottle of oxygen to be carried in order to revive the canary.

Now there are electronic devices that give warning of gas buildup, and sources of ignition are carefully avoided. Miners must wear special watches, all industrial equipment is spark free and the mine is mainly run on compressed air. There is no smoking on site, cellphones are banned and the lights are battery powered. Six-metre test drills are regularly made to reveal old workings before excavation is undertaken, and ventilation systems are much more efficient.

Stone dust (ground limestone) is sprayed through the tunnels to cover the top layer of coal dust, so that in the now unlikely event of an explosion the dust blown into the air will be non-combustible. The stone dust can be laid throughout, or there may be barriers built at strategic intervals. An explosion barrier consists of a series of stone-dust shelves or water-filled tubs suspended at intervals along the tunnels. In the event of an explosion the dust or water is propelled into the air, thus stopping the fire from spreading. The amount of stone dust required is proportional to the methane level, and the probability of a gas explosion generating a coal-dust explosion can be calculated with some accuracy to achieve a required standard.

If methane is present in significant volume it should be drained through a system of pipes before cutting occurs, or the walls of the tunnel may be sprayed with a concrete mixture in order to seal them. Generally the ventilation system is strong enough to keep the methane sufficiently diluted and to carry it outside the mine.

Miners each carry a self-rescuer, which can deliver them oxygen for 30 minutes – time enough, it is calculated, for them to reach one of the fresh-air bases located throughout the mine. In these bases, oxygen bottles and masks are stored, which should enable the men to reach the surface after an explosion. Finally, drug testing is regularly and randomly carried out and miners have to undergo a fitness test once a year, which includes walking out of the mine with respiration gear on.

Nevertheless, deaths still occur – 31 since I came to the Coast nine years ago. Apart from Pike there have been two individual deaths: one where a miner was drowned after breaking through into a flooded working, the other by a rockfall. In the early 1990s there were three deaths from a coal-face explosion. Before that there had been two major disasters locally: the Brunner explosion of 1896, killing 65 men; and the Strongman explosion of 1967, killing 19.

Both were found to have been caused by the incorrect setting of explosives. In the Strongman case a shot had been fired in such a way as to break through the face into an abandoned working where methane had built up. At Brunner a shot was fired the wrong way around, although there were also grumblings about poor ventilation.

There remains the problem of human frailty. As Darcy said on the night of the first Pike explosion: 'Someone did something stupid.'

Who controls the mine?

There have of course been significant technological changes in the way coal is extracted. The pick and shovel were little more than extensions of the human arm. Now, either coal cutters (road headers) bore out the coal, or high-pressure water blasts it out and loaders or conveyor belts or pipes carry it to the surface as a slurry. But explosives are still required to bore through the solid rock on the way to the coal, and sometimes to fragment the coal itself.

Despite changes in extractive methods and the tools available to read the dangers, the dangers have remained and not significantly changed. Health and safety continues to be a potent issue, for it calls into question control of the workplace.

There are three protagonists: the managers, the state and the employees. Management and employees regularly bargain over wages, but what about health and safety, which are part of the conditions of work?

There are issues of lighting, temperature, access to the mine and toilet provision. There is training of personnel and the planning of the tunnelling. There is the control of the considerable hazards – fire, explosion, rockfall, gas and ventilation; the standard of equipment and machinery, the provision of shafts; and the emergency response if something does go wrong.

Who has the final say on these matters? Should it be left to the employer? Should the state legislate minimum standards? In which case, how are these to be policed and what are the consequences of failure? How should the workforce be involved? There are any number of permutations and commutations, which have varied according to the ideological climate of the time.

Early on, the state simply wished to be notified if a mine was operating, and this was achieved through a licensing system. But the disasters at Kaitangata and Brunner produced public pressure for greater regulation. The Liberal government first elected in 1891 established a Department of Labour, which began to regulate working conditions across the workforce. Children were removed from factories; unions were given statutory protection; and significantly, in terms of Pike, 'check inspectors' were introduced into coalmines. These were worker representatives with the authority to inspect the safety of working conditions and to force management to improve those conditions if necessary. It meant a surrender of some management control. Department of Labour inspectors paid regular visits to ensure regulated standards were being met.

It was, as former New Zealand Council of Trade Unions (NZCTU) president Ross Wilson wrote in an article on health and safety in the *Labour History Project Journal*, 'a three-legged stool'.[36] Nevertheless, there were still problems, as the inquiry into the disaster at Ralph's mine in Huntly in 1914 revealed. The check inspector could become lazy, or overly friendly with management, and there was the perennial problem of the Department of Labour inspector ignoring his existence and liaising with management alone, for check inspectors were potentially invasive of the bureaucrat's territory.

Wilson states that 'historically, New Zealand followed the British model ... with minimum health and safety standards prescribed by quasi-criminal law and enforced by a Government inspectorate'. Union involvement could only take place by agreement with employers, the check inspectors in coalmines being the one exception.

He notes that in Britain in the 1970s there was a move away from legal enforcement of prescriptive standards toward general duty performance standards supported by elected worker health and safety representatives. This followed the Scandinavian model.

New Zealand rather slowly followed suit in the 1980s with a voluntary code suggested by a government advisory council, which also recommended a single act and an authority for workplace health and safety. In 1990 the Labour government introduced the Occupational Safety and Health Bill to cover these matters and to provide for elected health and safety reps in workplaces. But the ensuing National government stripped out these worker involvement provisions.

The general duty of the employer was to ensure health and safety in his or her workplace. If he failed in this duty he could be fined. Whereas prescriptive standards can be easily judged, general duty is more complex. Wilson notes that while the NZCTU supported the concept of legally enforced mandatory minimum standards, the organisation was sceptical that there was the political will to ensure that the act would be rigorously enforced.

There was further concern when previous existing acts and regulations were not consolidated into the new regulations and codes of practice under the 1992 act. The act also took away the right for workers in coalmines to elect check inspectors. With the Employment Contracts Act coming into force at the same time (1992), unions were rapidly disempowered and stripped of the right to worker health and safety representatives. It was the height of neo-liberal ideology, governed by two simplistic beliefs: (i) the employer, disciplined by market forces, should control the workplace; and (ii) workers are mere resources and the state has a minimalist role to play.

In 1999, with the government back in Labour's hands, the act was amended to restore the right of workers to elect health and safety representatives, and this was made mandatory for employers with 30 employees or more. There was also provision for training of these representatives.

But miners continued to pressure for a return to check inspectors and for there to be a mines inspectorate. Made up of experienced miners, this would be separate from the Department of Labour, which tended to be staffed by generalists who investigated workplace accidents after an accident had occurred. After two mining deaths in 2006 this pressure eventually led to a review. Submissions were summarised in a discussion paper in 2008, which suggested a number of possible additions to the performance-based framework.

A safety case regime would require employers to document their safety management systems and to gain approval from the department for these systems before they operate. But there was significant employer opposition to this idea, on the grounds that it would be too onerous on small operators, and that the department did not have sufficient resources to operate such a system without undue delay and costs to operators.

A further suggestion was to license 'high-risk activities'. There was some speculation as to what these activities might be, but they would include departures from the established standard – such as development work in gassy mines, introduction of new technology, and development through faulted ground. There proved to be little support for the idea as, once again, it increased the power and role of the state.

There was a suggestion that there be third-party monitoring of high-risk activities, with in some cases these activities being performed only under the supervision of an appropriately qualified person. While this was seen by some as being a useful provision for small operators, there was the problem of New Zealand having a small industrial base with already too few suitably qualified people.

There was general agreement that there should be a regulation requiring all operators to have a documented health and safety system and hazard management plan from the outset, and there was no antagonism to there being further approved codes of practices (ACOPS).

But when the unions argued for a reintroduction of check inspectors (in addition to health and safety representatives), who would inspect a mine every two weeks and who would have the authority to withdraw employees in hazardous circumstances, there was unanimous employer opposition (including at Pike River). Employers saw the role as confrontational, and claimed it would blur responsibility and create tension in the workplace. After all, the Health and Safety Act placed responsibility on employers, and check inspectors would reduce their authority. Accordingly, the Department of Labour made no significant changes from the review.[37]

With the Pike River disaster this decision has inevitably come under scrutiny, for before the explosion there had been numerous rumours among men who had worked there of health and safety issues: of significant gas, of an inexperienced workforce, of communication problems within a multinational workforce, of a negative response from management when problems were pointed out and of management being 'anti-union'.

These rumours were fleshed out in the first week of hearings of the royal commission in July 2011 when a picture was painted by Solid Energy CEO Don Elder[38] and geologist Jane Newman[39] of an undercapitalised company, managed by people unfamiliar with complex local conditions, failing to do sufficient research. Instead, they ploughed ahead with unrealistic expectations and encountered problems, which led to the need to earn some money earlier rather than later. They operated in a regulatory framework that put the onus on self-regulation, with the occasional inspection by a run-down, underfunded, inexperienced government department that might, in itself, be culpable for not closing down the mine. Training, under the new unit standards-based educational regime, had, in the opinion of former Inspector of Mines Harry Bell, become fragmented and uncertain.[40]

During the inquiry the list has continued to build: lack of toilets underground, no functioning fresh-air base, no satisfactory second egress, uncertain telephones, no regular trial evacuations, health and safety on the second tier of management and therefore (according to Health and Safety Manager Neville Rockhouse) not given due weight. And all this allowed by managers trained in the much tougher Australian model but becoming lax under the New Zealand system – because it allowed them to be.

If any good is to come out of the disaster, it will be at least a rectifying of this situation.

A key witness in stage three of the hearings was a Human Factors expert, Kathleen Callaghan, who had studied much of the evidence to that date. She identified that Pike was a start-up mine and a start-up company, both factors that increase risk. She noted that mining takes place in a harsh environment and is an industry that is associated with low-frequency, high-consequence events. The workforce had a high proportion of inexperienced men, involving workers from South Africa, Australia and Japan as well as New Zealand, speaking different languages and from different mining cultures, and this needed to be taken into account (but wasn't) when designing systems.

The hazard reports she studied were concerning because 'they document significant and recurring risks to safety in areas such as housekeeping, emergencies and ventilation … If you read them, they're those same things occurring time and time again.' She surmised that 'the problematic behaviour wasn't able to be controlled at managerial level'. Problems therefore were never rectified. There was a lack of communication and people were unable 'to lay their hands on important information'. From the human factor point of view, then, Pike River 'was an accident waiting to happen'.

Even more damningly, when she studied the paper trail she identified similar holes in the management culture of the Department of Labour.

'The holes that we identify, the errors, the error-producing conditions at Pike River mine are not dissimilar to the ones that are identified at the Department of Labour. They are very, very similar and I think we need to be mindful of that.'

Callaghan went on to say that this culture extended back to wider government. She quoted a relevant piece of folk wisdom – 'The fish rots from its head'– and demanded that the commission report in the widest manner possible:

> If we are to truly understand what happened at Pike River Mine
> and why it happened, for the purposes of trying to prevent a similar
> event in any industry in New Zealand happening again, we need to
> interrogate the strengths and weakness at all levels of the system and
> unless we clearly define the problem, any intervention is unlikely to
> be as efficacious and as efficient as it could be.

We can only hope, then, that the commission's report will put a final nail in the coffin of the neo-liberal health and safety regime.

Right: The Denniston Incline under construction. It opened in 1879.

S. C. Robertson collection

Below: The Denniston Plateau with the town under construction.

Alexander Turnbull Library

The living conditions in Denniston were basic – to say the least.

Right: The Brunner mine site was a bleak and dangerous place.

Alexander Turnbull Library

Below right: The single men's huts in Blackball are an example of the rudimentary accommodation in mining towns.

AJHR 1919, H44a, pp. 82–83

Below: A hard's day's work in the Blackball mine.

History House, Gremouth

Opposite page above: The aerial that carried coal from the Blackball mine to the railway at Ngahere in the early years of the 20th century: an example of the extensive infra-structure required to get coal to the marketplace.

Wood collection

Below: Blackball mine workers in about 1910, ready to start their shift.

Howett Collection, University of Canterbury Library

Above: Pat Hickey, a lead activist in the 1908 Blackball strike.

Alexander Turnbull Library

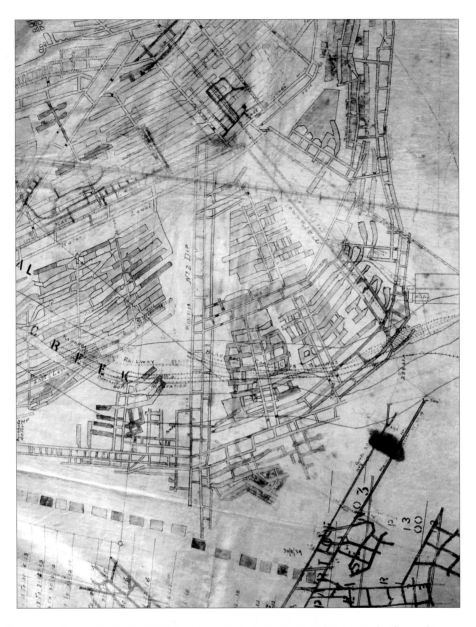

A map of the old Blackball mine, showing the extensive network of tunnels.

Jane Wells collection

Right: An anti-strike cartoon from the *Observer*, 14 March 1908. The caption read:
HIS HIGHNESS LABOUR
Chorus of Ministers: 'May it please Your Highness, we implore you not to strike. Bear patiently with the Arbitration Act a little longer, and, if it does not please Your Mightiness, we will amend it further so that it will please you.'

Auckland Public Library

Below: The Runanga Miners' Hall soon after it was built in 1908.

Alexander Turnbull Library

Above: The Leitch family at a picnic in Rapahoe. One brother was a mine manager and others were strikers in 1908.

Wood collection (donated by Selwyn Leitch)

Below: Guests heading toward the old Blackball mine during the 1908 Centennial Celebrations at Easter 2008.

Simon Ede

Above: The parade that formed part of the Blackball centennial celebrations.

Simon Ede

Below, left and right: Ventilation chimneys at the old Blackball mine are still extant.

Paul Maunder

Left: The entrance to the old Black-ball mine today.

Below: A sculpture by Phill Rooke (with an insert by Tony Manuel, Ngati Porou), which fronts the Blackball '08 memorial.

Above: The Lane Walker Rudkin factory in Greymouth was an example of the subsidised regional development that took place in the 1970s.

Cathy Allan

Below: The Lane Walker Rudkin Netball team. As well as providing employment, regional industry added to local social networks.

Cathy Allan

Above: Members of the crowd at the memorial service for the Pike River miners at the Omoto Racecourse, Greymouth, on 2 December 2010.

Stewart Nimmo

Below: A Pike River family at the tile-making session for the Workers' Memorial Wheel in Blackball: (from left) Joanne Palmer (Brendon Palmer's sister), her partner DJ, and Brendon's mother, Sheryll Palmer.

Above and below: The completed Workers' Memorial Wheel in Blackball, which features tiles made by the Pike River families.

Above: A young modern miner, Darcy Tuiavi'i, a hard rock tunneller at the Spring Creek mine.

Below: The Pike River family memorial at Atarau.

Above and below: Memorials to Stu Mudge and Milton Osborne: two of the 29 stones that make up the Pike family memorial at Atarau.

The main plaque of the memorial, which stands at the beginning of the road to the mine.

CHAPTER FOUR

Continuing the
Political Narrative

The spirit of 1908

A few weeks ago at the Working Men's Club a man from one of the families who have been in Blackball a couple of generations said to me, 'If you ever leave here, we'll cut down that thing over the road.' He was referring to Phill Rooke's sculpture celebrating the 1908 spirit. 'It's not Blackball,' he continued.

I didn't react to his threat for it seemed absurd. Instead, I studied his eyes, trying to penetrate to the consciousness that lay behind the anger, as he went on to tell me he'd always been a union man, but 'that's not about politics'. A bizarre statement, although joining a union can nowadays be seen as simply purchasing a service. Perhaps that was why he was angry about the sculpture, for it strongly negates that point of view.

And then he became conciliatory, as if regretting his outburst.

His threat took me back to another incident, when locals pulled down the Miners' Hall after the mine closed in 1967, because the hippies who had moved into town wanted to hold market days there. The hall wasn't a beautiful building but was very large and contained a story or two. However, certain old-timers in town got out their crowbars and demolished it. Out of spite? Out of rage? Out of envy of these long-haired blokes with their bra-less women? Out of fear of the approaching new age?

The community has experienced the changes from socialism to

reformism to mine closure and threatened death of the community, to consumerism, to neo-liberalism and postmodernism and the technological changes of the information revolution. What would a 1908 miner make of a Hilux and a chainsaw? Or a 42-inch LCD TV with SKY on which we watch species disappearing and real-time natural disasters?

Another scene at the Working Men's Club. We invited the Pike families to make a clay tile with the name of their man on it. The tiles would then be fired and glued to the rim of the wheel we had erected as a workers' memorial. They accepted the invitation enthusiastically; indeed, took over the project. As they arrived for the workshop, they had a sacred presence, unpretentious and vulnerable. Yet they were also aware of their collective strength. They hesitated in front of their piece of clay, frightened they'd get it wrong. 'I'm not arty-farty,' one said.

But after being shown a few simple techniques by Ian and Sue, the potters who live down the road toward Moana, they settled to the task. It turned out the family members appreciated being able to do something. Over the past months they had been talked to, talked about, given to, used by politicians, subjected to policies, experts … all well meaning enough, but this opportunity to exercise their subjectivity and make a small mark on the world was obviously therapeutic.

The whole project would cost no more than a grand, and the wheel now belongs, spiritually and emotionally, to the families. Somehow, with this group, there was continuity with the spirit of 1908.

Roller Coaster

What, in fact, happened to the union movement and working people after 1935?

First of all, the welfare state took the edge off class warfare. Workers previously had the lodge system, membership of which protected them and their families against the immediate shocks of hard times. The lodge system was controlled by the membership.

It was, if you like, part of libertarian socialism. Now the state took over the task.

Secondly, compulsory unionism took the guts out of the struggle. It meant many unionists were indifferent, even hostile to an organisation to which they were forced to belong. Unions became relatively wealthy and the workload of organisers (mainly the negotiation of a national agreement once a year) comfortable. To be secretary of a large union mainly made up of indifferent members (for example, the clerical workers) gave a considerable power base, as Trade Union Federation secretary Fintan Patrick Walsh, collaborator with the 'red-menace' scaremongering National government in 1951, well knew. And the activist unions (the wharfies, miners, seamen, freezing workers, carpenters and boilermakers) who threatened the cosy status quo could be dealt with from that base.

The union movement became tied to the Labour Party which, for a lengthy period post-World War II (with a couple of short breaks, the Norman Kirk years being the most notable), remained in opposition. Meanwhile, the communist movement was being blown apart by the winds of controversy – revelations of Stalin's brutality; revolts in Hungary, Czechoslovakia and Poland – which ended in the chaos of Mao's Cultural Revolution and the fall of the Berlin Wall.

During this period the New Zealand economy was doing well. Wolfgang Rosenberg writes:

> In the opinion of this writer, the term 'Economic Miracle' is appro-
> priately used for the development of the New Zealand economy
> between 1938 and 1975. Never before in the capitalist world has a
> country been able to maintain continuous unbroken and absolutely
> full employment for such a period of time ... During that time
> New Zealand showed that it was possible to exist within the Magic
> Square. This Magic Square consists of achieving the four goals of
> economic policy simultaneously:
>
> • Full employment
> • Balance of Payments equilibrium (the economy living within
>   its means)
> • Economic growth

- Relatively stable price levels.[41]

But then it began to unravel, as world commodity prices fell and Britain joined the European Union.

With the arrival of Roger Douglas and his neo-liberal henchmen the union movement became confused. Somehow, the fact that it was the Labour Party tearing apart the economic contract, and that some of its social policies were progressive, justified what was happening.

When National took over and brought in the Employment Contracts Act it removed the unions' previously accepted role in the social democratic system. National dealt some considerable blows to the welfare system as well. Suddenly all that workers had achieved in those early struggles was under threat. Meanwhile many broad left organisations had fragmented as feminists and Māori accused them of patriarchy and colonialism.

It was a revolution, but of another kind. In survival mode, unions amalgamated, lived off reserves built up in a previous period, and competed for (or poached) members. Some organisers went and worked for the bosses, and the union movement generally failed to offer support to the growing unemployed. A quaint concept of partnership was cobbled together by some unions in an attempt to survive within the neo-liberal regime. But very quickly union membership fell to 17 per cent of the workforce (much lower if you leave out public servants such as teachers and nurses).

Meanwhile the workforce had diversified, with many more women working by choice or out of necessity, and with the immigration of Pacific Islanders and other ethnic groups forming a low-wage labour pool. Jobs were increasingly offered in the form of short-term contracts, or as casual, on-call-type arrangements.

But there was another side to the coin. The rich were getting richer and flaunting their wealth so that the service industry became a lot busier. Those who owned property found their equity considerably increasing as house prices skyrocketed. Loans became readily available and cheap imports flooded the country, so that even low-income people could own what would once have been seen as a fancy car, fridge, TV and then computer.

Workers entered the state that cultural historian Raymond Williams calls 'private mobility'. It is exemplified by the sight of a student shifting flat with a trailerload of gear, or by the more substantial furniture van or shipping container of the nuclear family. It is the image of a mobile life whereby one increasingly moves around with the essential consumer items that go to make up one's personal equity, but also one's sense of identity. Individual consumer-based identities merge to form couples, even families, but can just as easily fragment to re-emerge in a new relationship or a reconstituted family, which has involved the splitting and merging of consumer items.

Loyalty to wider community organisations becomes fragile, except as they constitute systems of insurance against loss, such as trade unions.

The new mobile world is highly mediatised, as culture is penetrated by exchange values: the buying and selling and commodification of all human activity (including love, sex and family life), most clearly represented in commercials but extending to other cultural spheres. There have been various narratives describing this process, with general agreement about its underlying fascist tendencies. Raymond Williams, brought up in a Welsh coalmining village, describes the precarious and often desperate angst of the modernist artist being colonised by the corporate mass media:

> What we now have is a huge sector of capitalist-sponsored art, displayed in the polished routines of crime, fraud, intrigue, betrayal and gross degradation of sexuality ... This popular culture confirms the world's destructive inevitabilities.[42]

Frenchman Guy Debord writes equally sharply about the 'Society of the Spectacle', the spectacle being at 'the very heart of society's unreality',[43] for 'the spectacle proclaims the dominance of appearances and asserts that all human life, which is to say social life, is appearance.'[44]

For a bloke in Blackball, the arrival of a few hippies exploded into a digital invasion of otherness, attractively packaged with smiling faces and nubile bodies. He is surrounded today by diverse sexualities, different ethnic cultures, a growing number of tourists, Treaty of Waitangi claims and issues of conservation, accompanied by a growing surveillance by state bureaucrats.

Recent Coast history can, accordingly, be read as a narrative of betrayal: the closure of the mines, the dishonouring of the forestry accord, the tying up of land in national parks, the closure of schools, a health system in constant crisis, the poaching of talented kids by city schools, a lack of jobs for young people leading to an unbalanced population, and the inevitable battle with conservation groups when development is attempted.

And anyone who spends any time here quickly realises the difficulty of maintaining infrastructure because the sparse population is stretched along such a narrow ribbon of land, so that communities are separated by large distances.

The statistics, then, reveal a lower-than-average standard of education, a below-average income level, and the associated below-average health status. In short, statistically – and culturally – there is little difference between Coasters and Māori.

Betrayals

Those born and bred here, and who stay, have a notion of the indigenous. Being born and bred on the Coast is believed to impart special qualities associated with the landscape and the people. A Coaster is then:

- appreciative of nature because of living in close proximity to a unique landscape of river and forest, especially as a child;
- tenacious and tough, for that same landscape and associated wet climate can make life arduous;
- generous to neighbours and community;
- practical because engaged in physical work;
- suspicious of outsiders who want to change things;
- scornful of urban pretension;
- knowledgeable regarding the stories of the elders that tell of the living out of these qualities.

A single generation is sufficient to qualify one as 'indigenous', possibly because the truth of constant migration exists at least at the level of subtext. And of course these qualities, when associated with lack of education and poverty, can produce a redneck tendency. It leads to Barry Crump territory.

But this portrait of the born and bred Coaster bears little resemblance to those early miners, who were migrants forming close-knit, union-run communities and taking on the outside bosses from the basis of an internationally derived narrative of revolution. And unlike Angus McLagan's very clear analysis of the depression, couched in anti-capitalist terms, the economic and accompanying social narrative since the closing or downsizing of the coalmines is infused by a theme of betrayal by the workers' 'own' government. What are the facts?

As the local demand for coal diminished, the closure of some mines was inevitable. For those that remained open, a period of significant technological upgrading was required, and then the product refocused for the overseas smelting market. This process is seen as a betrayal, motivated by political revenge when National was in power, which continued in the corporatising of State Coal in 1987 and a further downsizing of the workforce. The fact that the latter was done by a Labour government remains unforgivable in Coasters' eyes. Les Neilson, who comes from a three-generation mining family, puts it like this:

> In 1987 a hundred-odd men got put off when it [State Coal] became Coal Corp. That was a pretty tragic time. I saw a lot of good men who opted for redundancy because they didn't want the stigma of being laid off. It was pretty demoralising. That was Douglas and Prebble. They had to change but it was poorly done. I was running the union at the time. I wrote the letter out when we [the miners' union] resigned from the Labour Party. It was the first time I saw a letter sent by email. To the Prime Minister. We never got a reply.

It meant that Les and his fellows were now in political limbo.

> It was a real kick in the guts for men who'd supported Labour all their lives. They treated them with contempt and that's never been forgotten. I think the party was hijacked. You've only got to see where Prebble and Douglas ended up – in the ACT Party. They were hijacked into the extreme right. That was a shocking time. It was

capitalism at its worst. Muldoon left the country in a mess, no doubt about that, but they could've treated people with dignity and respect. That was it for me. They'd shit on the workers.[45]

The scrapping of the forestry accord was seen as a further betrayal, for it was the Coast's 'Treaty'. The West Coast Accord[46] was signed in 1986 between the West Coast United Council, the Native Forests Action Council, Royal Forest and Bird Protection Society of New Zealand, Federated Mountain Clubs of New Zealand, the West Coast Timbers Association, the Westland Timber Workers' Union and the Crown. It was, in effect, a treaty between the Crown, the community (as represented by the local bodies), the timber industry, the unions and the conservation groups – a five-legged stool.

Its aim was to arrive at 'an overall strategy for West Coast forests'. As well as gazetting reserves and the Paparoa National Park, it provided for 'the allocation of sufficient indigenous production forest areas to make possible the maintenance, subject to competitive market forces, of the sawmilling on the West Coast at its current allowable level of cut, until exotic species become available in adequate quantity, *planned to be 2006 in Buller and between 1990 and 1995 in North Westland (except for Karamea for which adequate quantity is available at present level of allowable cut until at least 1994)*. The final part in italics was handwritten in after the conservation groups had signed the accord, and remained controversial.

Specific clauses then allowed for 200,000 hectares of forest to be designated as park and reserve; gave approval for the Pike River coalfield development to proceed; allowed current mining in reserve areas to continue; recommended the sale of state forest production areas to the Forestry Corporation; stated that the indigenous forests should be managed sustainably; required additional sensitivity in logging in South Westland; and required the remaining unclassified state forest to be controlled by the Department of Conservation.

This hard-won accord balanced the needs of the traditional native tree sawmilling industry to maintain plant and employment with the growing concerns of the conservation lobby – the Coast was the country's last significant remaining area of native forest.

There was to be a move to exotic plantations to supply the sawmills, but meanwhile logging of natives could continue under tight conditions. For example, in terms of beech forest, a single tree per hectare could be taken out by helicopter annually.

The gazetting of 80 per cent of the Coast's land area for reserve or national park was a significant victory for the conservation lobby. It is extraordinary to note that the Pike River coalfield was part of the deal, presumably allowed as a sweetener, for the locals were agreeing to the locking away of a substantial part of 'their land'. There is some similarity to Ngāi Tahu's original 'selling' of the Coast and retaining reserves, with coal replacing pounamu as the special resource.

But for the conservation lobby, any logging of native forest remained problematic. In 1991 the forest owners and the growing number of conservation groups met again to thrash out the New Zealand Forest Accord, which defined 'a native tree' and particularly focused on small stands of natives threatened by clearing for exotic plantations.

It was an area of growing controversy, and the newly elected Labour government of 1999 legislated away the 1986 West Coast Accord. As one critic put it:

> Timberlands West Coast Ltd [had] carefully planned for 10 years, at a cost of $3 million, with the guarantee of the West Coast Accord as a firm and contractually binding basis, to begin innovative and world-leading sustainable forest management processes and techniques for perpetual production of fine beech timber for furniture, and for enhanced conservation of threatened plants and wildlife in the process. The newly elected Labour government in December 1999 halted the environmental planning process, claiming that the support they [now had] from northern city electorates for a new policy to 'put a stop to all logging in state indigenous forests' was a valid mandate to break the 1986 contract with the West Coast region. Further, they decided to curtail the very successful, audited, sustainable management of rimu forests in South Westland that has been in operation for about 8 years, and have decided that it will end in 2002.[47]

There had been growing pressure: the Native Forest Action Group had exposed the National government's plans to expand logging and the lack of transparency in the Timberland's operation. As well, the logging of beech was revealed as economically problematic because of the long drying process required. Not trusting Timberlands, the protesters had resorted to direct action by sitting in trees (tree hugging), and a book by Nicky Hager[48] exposed the Shipley-led National government's secret machinations with Timberlands, which included setting up a 'citizens' lobby group'.

There remained controversy over the handwritten insertions in the original accord, and Labour had, as well, progressive urban electorate supporters to keep faith with. The conservation lobby had become numerically stronger and a seasoned political operator.

Support for Labour on the Coast slumped as 'their party' retook office in 1999. And Coasters were not particularly couth when it became clear the new government was going to jettison the West Coast Accord. Deputy Prime Minister Michael Cullen received a hostile reception in Greymouth during the 1999 election campaign, prompting Helen Clark's 'feral' comment.

In return for the closure of native logging in state-owned forests, the Coast was offered a capital sum of $120 million for economic development, to be run by a trust, and each council was given another $7 million for the same purposes. It was uncannily similar to the rationale behind the settling of Treaty of Waitangi claims: We take/took the land and give you some cash in return.

The ramifications of this policy decision have continued. The born and bred Coaster lobby remains bitter over this 'betrayal' and it fuelled a strong anti-Green sentiment ('Fertilise the forest – bury a Greenie' bumper stickers) that remains today.

Timberlands argued that it had developed a sustainable management model that was attracting worldwide interest, particularly from developing countries whose native forests were under threat. Whether the company was trustworthy was the question.

There were further layers of subtext, as revealed in the Native Forest Action Council's (NFAC) releases during the 1990s.[49] Coasters proudly noted that the forest down here has been preserved (unlike in the rest of the country) and that this proves they are conservationists at heart. The NFAC argued that this preservation was merely fortuitous. Due to the mountainous terrain, the wet climate and the poor underlying land quality, it was economically fruitless to clear much of the land. It has only been through the introduction of the technique of humping and hollowing (which is capital intensive and requires the modern digger) that much of the pakahi (swampy soil) is being turned into worthwhile dairying pasture. Because these circumstances overcame the usual 19th-century Pākehā drive to cut down every tree in sight, the West Coast forests survived.[50]

The NFAC argued that the real villain in terms of the Coast's economy was not the conservation cause but the neo-liberal insistence on the free play of market forces. Prior to free-market ideology being adopted, governments were attracted to the concept of regional economic development, and had been convinced that there should be no urban/rural divide. Development should be spread, to avoid undue pressure on infrastructure.

There was a policy during the 1970s, for example, of moving the offices of government departments to the regions, and there were grants and subsidies to encourage new industry in rural areas. Lane Walker Rudkin established clothing factories in Hokitika, Greymouth, Reefton and Westport, and PDL began manufacturing electrical components in Greymouth. Local industries were protected by tariffs and import controls, and the New Zealand dollar exchange rate was controlled to keep local products competitive on international markets. As a consequence, Lane Walker Rudkin provided 120 jobs in Greymouth alone. It meant the young could stay on the Coast instead of leaving to find work, and it meant that there was a mixed economy locally.

Of course economic change became necessary as the international market for agricultural products became less secure, but the New Zealand's government's approach in the second half of the 1980s was an ideologically pure policy of slash and burn. The development grants were cut, tariffs and import controls removed and the exchange rate floated. Ron Brierley, one of the new breed of entrepreneurs whom the new system encouraged, bought Lane Walker Rudkin, rationalised operations by closing down the regions, asset-stripped the company, began producing offshore to take advantage of cheap labour and eventually sold it off. End of the clothing industry on the Coast and in other rural areas. Another betrayal.

A further poignant case study is that of the pottery industry. As the 1960s 'alternative lifestyle' impulse spread, the craft of pottery flourished – it was handmade, non-factory, in touch with the earth, and therefore a cool thing to do. Many potters set up in rural areas because of cheap house prices. They could have a little land, with a garden and a goat, and be away from the rat race. They sold their mugs and plates and casserole dishes at the gate or through craft shops in town. The product was attractive, inexpensive and an alternative to the mass-produced – most New Zealand homes had a mug or two made locally. The potters didn't get rich but they got by, added diversity to the rural area in which they lived, became part of the community and sent their children to the local school. It was a worthwhile small-scale regional industry that spread across the country. Enter tariff-free neo-liberalism and the influx of cheap mass-produced goods from developing countries spelled the end of the pottery industry,[51] except for a few stalwarts like the couple who helped the Pike River families make their tiles.

Sometimes the linkages in this story fill me with pity and fear. Some genuinely tragic events have occurred in our society.

The charter of the West Coast Development Trust (now Development West Coast), set up to control the lump-sum 'treaty settlement', meant it remained under government control, with any significant expenditure requiring the approval of Wellington-appointed advisers.

It has basically limped along without clear direction or philosophy. A small business wanting a loan could, until recently, get the same loan, with fewer hoops to jump through, from its bank. Various direct investments by the trust have proved problematic; for example the Forever Beech factory, set up and pursued almost in a spirit of spite, has swallowed several millions with little return.

The trust has also been tardy in getting behind development projects like the proposed cycleway, and it has devoted a lot of energy to business development type workshops and promoting an entrepreneurial spirit among the young. It invested $1 million to pay some Auckland educationists to prove that literacy standards among West Coast primary pupils were on a par with the rest of the country – something local teachers could have told them for free.

It has also suffered from sectoral in-fighting and personality clashes, with mayors occasionally wanting to withdraw their region's share of the cake. But that could be equally unrewarding, with two of the councils blowing their treaty spoils on failed projects: surfboard manufacturing in Westland and a sock factory in Buller.

The problem is that in a neo-liberal economy, regional economic development and the associated job creation are very difficult. If it fits the market, a sector doesn't require assistance. Mining and dairying have market fit, as does tourism. But manufacturing is tough and generally in decline throughout the country. Manufacturing was the sector that successive neo-liberal governments gave away in return for access for New Zealand's agricultural products.

Tiriti problems

In terms of local race relations there are further contradictions, felt as betrayals on both sides. Despite there being some affinities between Pākehā and Māori as fellow Coasters in terms of relationship with land and this community, there are some tensions resulting from the sorry saga of the administration of Māori reserve land in Greymouth.

When local Māori 'sold' the seven million acres of the West Coast to the Crown in 1856 for £300, the tangata whenua retained the Arahura River block (the sacred source of pounamu), and the land on which the commercial centre of Greymouth and its inner suburbs now lie, which was the site of their major settlement.

Ten years later, faced with the gold rush and huge pressure for land in Greymouth, the rūnanga asked the Crown to administer the land on its behalf. In the intervening decade the rūnanga itself had leased some sections of land to Pākehā, but didn't have the resources to deal with the chaos of the gold rush. The Crown took over the land administration and developed and leased out sections. But during the next two decades there was constant agitation by Pākehā leaseholders for their land to be made freehold. There was, and remains, in New Zealand, a deep antagonism to the uncertainties of leased land, especially regarding the problem of getting back the value of improvements when the lease is given up.

The Crown duly 'resolved' the problem in 1887 with legislation that gave leaseholders a perpetual lease.[52] But it had forgotten to consult local Māori. When Ngāi Tahu took this issue to the Waitangi Tribunal a century later in 1991, Tipene O'Regan stated that this act constituted an under-the-table form of confiscation.[53] At the time, Māori would have been agreeable to a 63-year lease, with the right of renewal for a further 63 years, but not to leases in perpetuity, which meant giving up the land forever. O'Regan further argued that this has meant that Māori, deprived of the use of their land, have been unable to earn a living on the Coast and have had to move away. This constituted a legal, cultural and economic betrayal of Māori – a not uncommon event.

After 1887 the Crown administrator reviewed rents every 21 years and the rents were kept below market rates – so much so that the tribe considered the money lost would constitute an unrealistic claim to government.

In 1955 a further act of parliament set the leases at 4 per cent of the land value, but retained the 21-year review period. The rampant inflation of the 1960s and 1970s meant a growing drop in the rate of return. And then in 1967 a further act allowed lessees to purchase the land freehold from the Māori Trustee.

As a result of growing Māori pressure a 1973 royal commission recommended five-yearly rent reviews, and that rents be fixed at 1 per cent above the return on government stock. It also recommended that the Māori owners take over the administration. Accordingly, in 1976 the Mawhera Incorporation was born through a further act of parliament that also repealed the tenants' right to freehold the land. The legislation introduced rent review periods of five years for commercial properties and seven years for residential.

The Mawhera Incorporation was made up of members of those families who could whakapapa back to the families who signed the deed of sale in 1856.[54] The incorporation administered 500 sections in Greymouth – half of them commercial, the rest residential. But the rental return remained below market value; for example in 1987 the gross return was 1.95 per cent when a reasonable return would have been in the vicinity of 10 per cent.

Finally, in 1997, a further act compensated Mawhera for past losses – to the tune of $9 million – and also compensated tenants for the inevitable future rent rises. A five-year transition period was set for the move to market rentals, which duly arrived in 2004. Since then the rents have skyrocketed – for example from $6000 to $22,000 for one commercial property – with rents on private sections escalating to the $100 a week mark. With the leaseholder also having to pay the rates, the outgoings became a significant amount for a small business or a householder on a low income. The sum continues to rise but, unlike a mortgage, is never actually paid off. Accordingly, the sale price of houses on leasehold land has plummeted, often to below $100,000. This has fuelled anti-Māori sentiment among the mainly Pākehā leaseholders.

There had been in the past an appreciation on both sides that, given the leases in perpetuity, improvement in the commercial sector was mutually advantageous. But lately Mawhera has taken a hard-nosed approach, driven by a justifiable sense of past grievance. The corporation itself, as a capitalist venture, has moved from a mass shareholding venture (as individual members have sold their shares) to become focused on two family trusts: Te Maraki Ellison Toroa Whānau (with 135,000 shares) and the Mason Family (100,000 shares), with its elder, Maika Mason, personally owning another 100,000. This has resulted in a trinity of doubtful actions that have soured race relations.[55]

In the mid-1990s the increase in the land rental forced the Greymouth Uniting Church to decide it could no longer afford to keep its building, which was of considerable heritage value. The church was offered to the council, which declined, and the building was then put on the open market. Mawhera bought it and its developer (Christchurch entrepreneur Hugh Pavletich) onsold it to Caltex as a service station site. This required demolition of the church building, much to the grief of many locals, including a recently established heritage group.

In 2008 Mawhera removed a war memorial gateway without consultation with the community, as it was subject to a Historic Places Trust classification that could have been problematic to subsequent development. Then in 2010 the Mawhera Incorporation increased the rental on the trotting club land so that the club was forced to vacate Greymouth's raceway, which now lies increasingly derelict. Mawhera has plans for a shopping mall development on the land, which would threaten the existing business district, but in the current climate that seems unlikely to go ahead. Nor are Mawhera's actions approved of by many Māori locals, be they tangata whenua who do not belong to the scheme, or Māori from outside the area. The Mawhera Incorporation thus far has contributed little to local causes.

When anger at historical grievances is focused on a current generation of Pākehā with little knowledge or felt ownership of those wrongs, then trouble is certain to arise. There seems, as well, little logic in creating a slum out of the central business district, or chasing it away to non-leasehold land. What would Mawhera then do with Greymouth? The grievance based on past injustice has become infused with capitalist entrepreneurial energy and this is the sort of emotional mix that in more extreme circumstances degenerates into an ethnic cleansing scenario, unless reasoned and reasoning heads intervene. Meanwhile the situation prevents the Coast from undertaking the journeys of reconciliation that have occurred in many North Island centres.

Papatūānuku

This difficult history since the 1960s – almost a neo-colonial period, even with some ethnic clashes – including a long period of significant unemployment, means that many on the Coast have fixed ideas when it comes to facing the problems of the new century, in particular the issues of climate change and conservation. In a way, the depth of grieving that the Pike River disaster has caused seems related to the fact that that mine was the original carrot offered to Coasters in return for locking up the forests into national park. Now, as Reefton painter Alison Hale said to me recently, 'The earth itself seems to have spoken.'

CHAPTER FIVE

Climate Change

M uch West Coast art focuses on the landscape, especially celebrating the nikau palms that adorn the coastal fringe around
Punakaiki. It is, through this lens, a people-less place.

Reefton artist Alison Hale is a notable exception. She worked
on farms and as a factory worker at Lane Walker Rudkin before
training in art at the local polytechnic. Many of her paintings are
of horses and their anonymous riders in a rain-drenched landscape,
both man and beast appearing elongated, unformed, with maybe an
industrial ruin as backdrop. They strike a chord, as human civilisa-
tion is tentative and often solitary on the Coast. But Hale paints
whitebait and trout as well – underwater images that are much
clearer and more coherent.

The Pike River disaster inspired a more cogent image of human
social life. On the back cover of this book is Hale's painting of a
pregnant woman and her two children scanning the Paparoa Range
in which the coalmine is located, looking for their man to return. It
is an evocative image of loss in an unforgiving and indifferent land,
reminiscent of the dustbowl rural portraits of depression America,
and an image that is a suitable backdrop for this chapter in which,
given the current environmental crisis, it is necessary to focus on
the future role of coal.

Leave it in the ground?

With the alarming consequences of fossil fuel-provoked climate change: massive species loss, extreme weather events, rising sea levels, dead oceans and calamitous suffering for the people in many countries of the world, and with coal being the dirtiest of fossil fuels in terms of CO_2 emissions and toxic waste, the environmentalists' call to 'leave it in the ground' is gaining political traction. This is in fact current Green Party policy (once existing mines run their course), and coal-powered power stations are being targeted by environmental activists in the US, Britain and Australia. As well, younger generations are increasingly environmentally focused. It was schoolchildren who finally persuaded the Grey District Council to introduce recycling.

The debate in the US, which generates 48 per cent of its electricity in coal-powered stations, is particularly volatile. But China and India are fuelling their industrial revolutions with coal, so that worldwide coal use grew by 22 per cent between 2002 and 2007. This same period saw a rise of 3 per cent in CO_2 emissions. With the predicted growth of the world's population from seven to nine billion by 2030 and an expected 50 per cent increase in energy demand, the use of coal is likely to increase rather than diminish.[56] Yet slowing climate change is fundamental to the survival of human society as we know it.

As it has come under attack, the coal industry has responded with a 'clean coal' campaign, which is focused on developing carbon capture and storage technology and its implementation (CCS). After the protests of the 1980s, power stations generally now scrub the emissions of sulphur compounds and capture the smaller particles that were the source of acid rain and atmospheric irritants. But capturing (sequestering) the CO_2 is a more complex matter.

There are two techniques. One is to burn the coal in a series of environments beginning with a pure oxygen chamber, out of which process is produced hydrogen (a favoured fuel that is seen as eventually replacing petrol and diesel) and pure CO_2. The other process is to mix the emissions with an ammonia-based solution that captures the CO^2. This solution is further treated to release the CO^2, with the ammonia solution then being recycled. In both cases the captured CO^2 is subsequently piped (with sometimes a necessary transport stage) deep down into the earth, where it is stored in porous rock or pockets of saline solution that are capped by layers of non-porous rock. Once the vent is sealed the CO^2 will remain trapped, according to CCS advocates, sometimes undergoing further chemical changes that render it even more stable.[57] However, some critics remain sceptical, suggesting the increased pressure could well crumble the porous rock.

The suitable storage sites across the globe are discrete, lasting to the middle of the century if most CO^2 is captured between now and then. Both CCS processes significantly increase the price of coal-generated power, but, it is argued, they allow coal to continue to be ethically used as a necessary transition fuel, especially given the inevitable ongoing use of the material by the emerging Asian economies. This argument gained traction with the recent nuclear power station disaster in Japan, which has highlighted the danger of nuclear material.

This line of argument is of course well funded by the coal industry, but has also been accepted by EU groupings such as the CCS network and the Zero Emissions Platform (ZEP),[58] as well as corporate networks such as the Global CCS Institute. A variety of trials is currently under way, but the technology is not yet in widespread use. Nor is it totally proven.

The renewable lobby is smaller in scale, non-centrist and alternative, as generally characterises the grassroots climate change movement. So we see two models of power generation: one centred on large power stations, the other on a network of dispersed generation types: solar panels, wind turbines, wave generation, micro-hydro schemes and so on. These models can be seen as political metaphors, the one generating a centrist, authoritarian society, the other a diverse, democratic society.

The Wuppertal Institute for Climate, Environment and Energy has produced a report for the German Federal Ministry for the Environment, Nature Conservation and Nuclear Safety (BMU).[59]

Entitled *Comparisons of Renewable Energy Technologies with Carbon Dioxide Capture and Storage (CCS)*, it is, according to the website, 'one of the most in depth documents to enter the public domain on this controversial subject'. The authors write:

> While many are of the opinion that there is no reason why CCS cannot be employed alongside emerging renewable technologies, the fact remains that both are in competition for scarce resources and funding. As a result, supporting one of the two impedes the development and deployment of the other.

Perhaps the single most significant conclusion of the report is its estimate of the potential quantity of CO^2 that can be sequestered in Europe. The authors put this as equivalent to just 40 years of the continent's current annual CO^2 emissions from large power sources (around 49 billion tonnes).

When one considers the huge cost of a substantial pipeline network and the other infrastructure required to transport the greenhouse gas to its final location (typically under the North Sea), this raises considerable questions regarding the attractiveness of CCS as a low-carbon option.

The report also makes the case that CCS is still the highest-carbon of low-carbon technologies, once its full life-cycle is considered, particularly as a result of the increase in coal consumption that would be required to meet current energy demand. This means it has a much higher overall environmental impact than renewable technologies – in the form of air pollution from both coal combustion and shipping the coal to the plant, and the damage done by mining operations. Once all upstream processes are taken into consideration, the authors of the report state that CCS has the potential of reducing emissions from power plants commencing operations in 2020 by 68–87 per cent (rising to 95 per cent in exceptional cases).

However, the authors estimate that in 2025, offshore wind, solar, thermal and photovoltaics will generate, respectively, only 5–8 per cent, 11–18 per cent and 14–24 per cent of the emissions from CCS plants.

They also make the point that the dynamics of the expansion of renewables in the electricity sector remain high. It is possible that individual renewable energy technologies may be able to compete with CCS power plants in terms of output as early as 2020. Barbara Freese, arguing along similar lines, points to a cultural impediment in refitting coal:

> Today, though, the thrill of coal is largely gone, and it's not likely to come back, even if technological breakthroughs can reduce its environmental impact. Bright, ambitious people eager to change the world will be less inspired by the challenge of building a vast new carbon sequestration infrastructure – essentially a system of perpetual waste management – than by the challenge of building completely new energy systems with no waste at all. Enthusiasm and talent will flow more freely to the new energy industries, not to mention the backing of visionary financiers and environmentally concerned investors. Most people would simply rather direct their passion and money toward creating a new world rather than toward retrofitting the old one …[60]

One thing is certain: coal is on the way out as a power generator. It may survive as a transition fuel, but within 50-odd years it will be redundant. How will this affect New Zealand – and more particularly the West Coast?

The local debate

In New Zealand electricity generation, the coal-fuelled Huntly Power Station operates as a peak-hour supplier and is capable of producing 25 per cent of the country's power requirements. But when Mighty River Power tried to turn Marsden Point 2 into a further coal-fuelled generator, environmentalists won the day. Question: Is it worth retrofitting Huntly?

Another debate is taking place around Solid Energy's wish to convert low-grade lignite deposits into diesel, urea or briquettes. The arguments for doing so, presented at a recent conference by Solid Energy chief executive officer Don Elder, were not unpersuasive.[61] New Zealand could produce its own diesel for the next 500 years and be equally independent in terms of nitrogen-based fertiliser. Otherwise we will be at the mercy of overseas producers, and with peak oil coming, the costs will drastically rise. We can capture the CO_2 and there are suitable sites in Southland to store it.

Yet open-cast mining of low-quality coal is likely to be as environmentally ugly as the mining of tar sands in Canada, described by one protester as 'scraping the bottom of the barrel'. And unless we change our neo-liberal economic model, producing these items here is not going to benefit New Zealanders in terms of cost (other than by reducing transport miles), for the world market price will be charged, as it now is for meat and milk products. The Green alternative would be to develop non-fossil fuel transport systems and organic agriculture, noting that organic products are high value on any market. This debate is beginning in New Zealand, but the tar-sands protests are becoming huge as they move to the US. The mining of low-grade fossil-fuel deposits is therefore dangerous political country, and Elder has changed tack somewhat opportunistically. Five years ago he was advocating the Southland deposits be used for electricity generation.

Some coal on the Coast is used for heating households, swimming pools, dairy factories and the like, and the pressure will mount in terms of this usage. But most of the coal mined is high-grade bituminous coal exported for smelting purposes in Europe, Asia and South America. This was the proposed market for Pike River coal (although there seems to be some doubt as to the quality of the first batches of coal produced from the mine).[62]

It seems unlikely that another smelting method for steel will be found and it would seem environmentally valid for the coal to continue to be mined for this purpose, if the CO_2 produced in the smelting process is captured. It is here that the environmentalist position becomes theological rather than pragmatic. There is a steel component in the concrete floor of the eco-friendly house, in the wind turbine, in the hydro-electric scheme, in the electric car, and certainly in the railway (to be preferred over the private car or trucking). As Spring Creek miner Les Neilson stated during his interview:

> The Greens wouldn't have a glass to drink out of without mining.

Certainly wouldn't have a car or an aeroplane. They'd have nothing. We'd be back to the stone age. The sad part about mining is you can't do it without digging a hole somewhere.[63]

The current Green Party position is a compromise between the fundamentalists, who would stop coalmining now, and the realists. It allows existing mines to continue to work out their natural life, but no new mines to be developed. West Coast-based Green list MP Kevin Hague explains:

> If the coal is being mined to burn it, then internationally, that is the single biggest driver of climate change. We can't afford to keep doing it. With coalmining as a major part of our economy and culture, we need to be doing the transition now. So starting new coalmines is mindless.[64]

Allowing existing mines to keep operating is pragmatic. 'There are right now a whole bunch of people who make their living mining coal. And on the Coast the alternative industries pay a lot less.'

He points out, however, that the actual number of Coasters mining is small, with a lot of the workers coming from elsewhere, sometimes temporarily. If mining stopped, they would move on.

> The reason we're saying keep the existing mines open is largely about providing certainty for the local people currently working in the mines. So for people in their fifties, [where] mining is the only thing they've ever done, they need to have certainty.

Within this scheme, if it were to become law, there is a grey area in terms of defining 'existing mines'. Solid Energy is developing a new mine for the same seam at Spring Creek. Would this be considered a new mine, or an extension of the existing one?

In terms of the validity of coal continuing to be used for smelting steel, Hague says he has not researched the issue, but is keen for different uses of coal to be explored. 'I have this idea — could you make carbon fibre? I don't know the answer. The world is going to need alternatives to plastics. Within 10 years the cost of plastic will be prohibitive.'

He points out as well that coalmining, while currently paying high wages because of the international demand for miners, does not lead to regional wealth, which would balance the environmental damage and the risk of the work.

> I guess Pike is just the latest of a string of mining disasters that illustrates the risk. And we don't get the wealth. Typically it goes somewhere else. When I look around the world I can't see a community that has mining as its mainstay that anyone would describe as a wealthy community. So the transition to another sort of economy is pressing and also desirable.

But the shape of such an economy is unclear. Hague makes the call for locally produced food:

> Why not grow our food locally, with a short supply chain? It would be healthier food and a good deal for the growers. We would see a better status for people growing food. There are also other goods and services that should be locally sourced.

All well and good, but with a marketplace of 30,000 people it is not a big industry. And then there is the usual call to add value to local resources, especially wood products.

> We need to look at manufacturing. It mightn't mean producing industrial goods, but processing timber etc. That's why I'm interested in making carbon fibre out of high-grade coal. I wish Development West Coast would get involved in this task, rather than looking backward.

He is aware of the need to change the system in order for this to be feasible:

> I believe in setting import controls and controlling exchange rates. These would take us out of the neo-liberal paradigm. This would make us similar to Denmark. Twenty years ago Denmark had an economy very like New Zealand's. What they did was invest a lot of government money into R&D on sustainable energy and as a result Denmark is now *the* manufacturer and exporter of wind turbine technology – and they're a country similar in size [to New Zealand]. There are a lot of parallels.

It is part realism, part wishful thinking – at this stage. For me, the Greens need to be more detailed in their analysis: to demand

CCS at Huntly and at other plants using coal generation. If that is not economic, then such plants should switch to sustainable energy. They should continue to question the lignite development, but need to accept the production of high-quality coking coal.

But it is important for the Coast as well to become less 'theological' and not simply preach that all mining is good. The region needs to articulate its own environmental position and acknowledge past mistakes. As Les Neilson states:

> Strongman No 2 was an absolute disaster. There've been some bad things done, but you look at goldmining – look at the Croesus Track. I've seen comments in the [visitors'] book up there of how nice it is to drive through the virgin bush, but it was all mined up there, so things change. Some of our nicest areas are ex-mining.

And there is a willingness to rectify mistakes. Sulphurous water leaches out of the old Blackball mine into a nearby creek, killing all life in the creek. Neilson is going to try to fix that.

> With the Blackball mine we're gonna have a go at stopping the water running out of there. There's an old water-race tunnel. It won't be as easy as just plugging it up – it might come out further up then. We'll have to block the other tunnels as well with good solid concrete. It's worth a go.

A future economy

It is necessary to accept Hague's imperative to look at a transition economy for the Coast, based on the understanding that coal (like gold) is a limited resource. This could lead to a demand that we mine the high-quality coal more slowly, leading to a more sustainable lifestyle for the current miner, to a reduction of the frenetic capitalist merry-go-round; and that as we more slowly work our way through this valuable resource, we plan a future West Coast. The leading questions are: How do we replace these well-paid jobs? What can we produce down here that can overcome the neo-liberal barriers to remote area manufacturing?

As Hague suggests, this should surely be the primary focus of Development West Coast: to begin to research, to pilot and then oversee this transition. Because 50 years is in fact quite a short time

– little more than a single working life. And there is every reason for a corporation like Solid Energy to be involved in the discussion.

Tourism could well diminish. Already people are becoming concerned about their individual carbon footprint and 'unnecessary' air travel is frowned upon. It is also likely that the cost of air travel will increase. Should we be examining the type of tourism we provide on the Coast? In Hague's view, 'Tourism that is based on putting people on a bus for a week is stupid. The smart way is to keep people in a place for longer. For example, a place like Wilderness Lodge pays good wages and provides scientifically oriented excursions etc.'

There are glimmers of a less mining-focused Coast: dairying, tourism, DOC, lifestyle artists and craftspeople (some of whom specialise in working local materials such as pounamu), organic food growing, processed meats, forestry, whitebait, taking advantage of micro-climates for food growing, micro-hydro schemes, holding the past through museums and festivals … and many jobs today mean you can live anywhere. Hague again:

> Different ways of participating in the economy are developing among younger people. I know people who live on the Coast but work in a place that doesn't have any physical location. Or has a physical place that is nominal. Those jobs tend to be well paid. A variety of IT jobs, but quite a range. Customer service jobs, for example.

The Gloriavale Christian Community in the Haupiri Valley offers an interesting example of value-based alternative living. If one sees past its creationist and patriarchal ideology and the social dramas that all communal living produces, its achievements are considerable. The community supports over 400 people, runs its own pre-schools and schools, pays for the training of its own health workers, teachers, engineers and vets, runs very successful business enterprises including a dairy farm and a value-added sphagnum moss export company, has ventured into high-value tourism and runs its own aid programme in India. It skilfully interleaves with the state system and contributes generously to the local community. Of course its economic success owes a great deal to a non-wage economy, but as a transition model it is not to be dismissed, and certainly challenges those of radical inclination to test their collective values in practice.

What is certain is that without focused planning, the Coast is doomed over the next 50 years to the continuing betrayals of any Third World economy, with its valuable resources being exploited by outside capital, with only a lucky few locals nibbling the cake. And then it will be faced with a crisis of falling population and reduced infrastructure.

In terms of beginning this planning process, with three small parochial councils there is a problem with developing a unified political voice and effective leadership. The national electoral boundary takes in Tasman and Golden Bay, with their very different population of orchardists and ex-pat Germans, so that the Coast voice is significantly diluted. The local paper is short on analysis and there is a lack of issue-based community organisation past the various caregiving non-governmental organisations. Coasters tend to be told what to do rather than make their own demands and decisions.

Yet the collective action of the Pike River families gives some hope. They demanded that the hearings be held in Greymouth, they demanded proper representation, they have developed a strong, unified media presence, they have maintained internal discipline, they have good relations with the union and they have presented simple yet valid demands.

The 29 remain entombed. How long before they are retrieved? For in a way they have become a symbol of the future.

CHAPTER SIX

The Modern Miner

In this chapter I search for continuity and note the changes between past and present mining traditions. The content comes from interviews and knowledge gained through friendships.

An old-timer

Les Neilson was born in Blackball in 1944. His father was a miner, as was his grandfather. The family came from Scotland in the late 19th century to chase the gold. From the Australian goldfields they moved to Ross, the goldfield south of Hokitika. But with 15 children and the need to find work for all the boys they moved to the larger Blackball. Coal was on the up; gold was going down. Les's father was born in 1903 and started in the mine after the war. Four of his brothers fought at Gallipoli.

As a child, Les remembers Blackball being a busy town of 1000 or more people, with about 200 working in the mine. With the dredge on the creek below the town, the train arriving and departing and the sawmills operating it was a noisy place, but everyone got used to it. 'We couldn't sleep if it was silent,' Les recalls. His time at Blackball School was one of the best times in his life – 'everyone was equal'. Tuition was good and he was top of the class – and top in sport. At night all the kids would practise league on the domain. 'There'd be a hundred people down there.' The town was divided into two geographical groups – 'the up-towners and the down-towners'. There were pictures on a Saturday night, with the little kids in the front row half wishing they were home in bed.

The annual miners' picnic was the highlight of the year. Twelve railway carriages would take the town's inhabitants down to Lake Mahinapua. The day before, all the fathers had made little painted paper windmills for their kids and they'd hang these out the windows of the train. The union gave each child 2/6d to spend at the picnic – quite a large sum of money. There was a doctor in town – the men wouldn't go to work without one present, everyone voted Labour and all the men belonged to the union. Les remembers crying when Prime Minister Peter Fraser died.

He trained as a builder and worked outside the mining industry for a period before getting a job at Rewanui (near Runanga) as a fitter. They did all the jobs in the mine that the hewers and truckers didn't do – retrofitting sets when the roof started to crack, laying rails and so on. He was used to being underground because when he was a child his father used to take him down the mine at weekends to walk their dog. The dog would chase rats and, being low to the ground, would sometimes hit a patch of 'coal damp' (a mix of CO_2 and nitrogen) and collapse for lack of air. His father would pick him up and 'play him like the bagpipes' – pushing air into the dog's lungs. Then he'd be off again. Les tells this story when he lectures on gas in the mines.

Les continued working through the 'Rogernomics' period of downsizing. He was union delegate at the time but left the Labour Party in protest, as we have seen, and has been in political limbo ever since. He's been through the technological changes, from hewer and trucker to scraper, to hydro-mining – the use of high-pressure water to wash out the coal. The latter he considers a blessing, for it makes the job a lot safer. Taking down the tops (the roof) with a pick was always dangerous.

The generation of miners that produced Les was almost tribal: extended family living in the one place, doing the same job and sharing the same stories. I asked him whether he thought there was continuity between past and present miners.

No, not really. It's changed so much. When I first started in the mines everyone grew up in mining communities. Now we've got people from everywhere, jokers who know nothing about the history of it. We were brought up with the history, it was father-to-son sort of thing. Now jokers don't really care too much about it. When something goes wrong, the union gets brought to the fore at that stage. Like it strengthened up after Pike River. A lot of them wouldn't even be in the union unless it was a standardised thing.

Les sees a change of values, for miners are in a higher wage bracket now:

The average blokes are getting 60 or 70 grand. A lot of them are getting over 100 grand, whereas the [national] average wage is probably only 25 grand. It puts them in a different class. But they deserve the good money. The shift work makes it a terrible job.

In the old days there were two shifts, with weekends free. But now it's round the clock, seven days a week. That destroys social lives. I think it destroys family life in a lot of ways. So the only real advantage is the pay packets. They don't have the same care as they used to have. Years ago when the hewers had their own face to work with, they took a lot of pride in their workmanship. Now it's only machines, so it's a monotonous sort of job. They end up zombies waiting for their days off. It destroys family life, football for young kids and so on. If one of them is having a party he can take the day off, but he can't invite all his mates, because they've got to work. Soul destroying.

But there seems no way to go back to the good old days.

I don't know how you get back to the eight-hour day. Can the workers rise up again? I don't think there's any need for the 24/7 thing – you've only got a finite resource, you're better to take your time. At Stockton they're ripping out the resource at a great rate – [but] we haven't got that much quality coal.

Les sees the modern miners as men coming from 'all over the place' for the money, without awareness of the history, using the union as an insurance policy, working for an industry that is ripping out a non-renewable resource with giant machinery as fast as possible. He could be accused of nostalgia, which is characterised by the editors of a new study of working-class heritage as 'an insatiable yearning' that 'cherishes the romantic memory of a time when the working class could more easily produce its own meaningful world-view: the unproblematic community of the "general interest".'[65]

English authors in the same study contrast 'Englishness' with 'Britishness' – the former belonging culturally to the old England, whereas the latter characterises the new Blairite, multicultural Britain.[66] On the Coast the same dichotomy could be drawn between the 'tribal' miner of Les's day and the new globalised worker, or even the treaty-educated New Zealand worker from the north, arriving here for the money. Is this a true picture or another mystification? I interviewed a couple of young miners who have moved here from outside the area.

Newcomer

Darcy Tuiavi'i is Samoan/Māori, brought up by his mother's Samoan family, with whom he identifies.[67] As a child it meant spending a lot of time at church, plus attending family get-togethers every Sunday, at Easter and Christmas and so on. The extended family was a very real presence. They didn't have much money but were proud of being Samoan. By the time he got to school the level of racism had diminished but was still present: 'Always if something goes missing, it's interrogate the Islander or the Māori. If you walk into the dairy wearing a hoodie, they'll ask you to take your hat off.'

In fact that happened to him recently at the Warehouse in Greymouth:

> I was wearing my hoodie: it was half on – I'd just had a haircut and
> it was raining and I walked in and the security woman comes up
> and asks me to take my hat off. I ask her why and she says, Just so
> we can see your face. I said to her, You going to ask those other three
> [Pākehā] guys there to take off theirs?

These incidents understandably create anger, which he has learned to control. So his early life was characterised by economic hardship, extended family and racism. This impacted on his performance at school, and English was hard past a certain level. There was the getting into trouble, especially fighting with the

Māori kids, plus a bit of harassment from the police, and also a lack of help with study.

> My grandmother couldn't do much, her English was broken as. Helen [his aunt] was there but she was studying at the time to become a nurse. My real Mum was doing shift work, she was never there. Her husband was working as well. Someone else would come around and look after us, so homework never got done – stuff like that.

He left school to join a sports academy. 'I used to play league in Aussie and I always had this dream of being a famous rugby player, or league player, but that dream died as I got older.' The academy was good but he began to lose focus and just scraped by with the academic work, so he left and had a year in Sydney. He 'scored' a job delivering gib board to building sites. He had two cousins working for the company and they arranged it with the boss. It was not well paid, but it was more money than he was used to having. That tends to be a norm for Samoans – they get a job with a firm where relatives are working.

Darcy came back to Wellington and joined up with Allied Labour Hire. They sent him to a scaffolding company which then offered him a job. This was his first foot on the ladder:

> ACROW [the scaffolding company] was really good. They looked after me pretty well. I did three years there. The only trouble was doing the qualifications. They kept getting put off because more work came on. But this was an actual trade and I was getting somewhere for the first time. I was proud of being a scaffolder. The guys I was working with – the majority were Islanders and Māori – they were proud. For them it was quite an achievement. We liked coming to work.

But because of high house prices in Wellington, he and his partner (my daughter) bought a house in Blackball – it was affordable and later, when they have kids, they'll be able to live for a time on one wage. Darcy got a job with a Spring Creek contractor, Geotech.

> I came down for the interviews, did my training, moved down here

and next day I was working underground. Moving down here I wondered what I was doing – you know, leaving my family. But once I got into work mode I started to enjoy myself. New things keep you interested. We began working machinery. That was a new thing for me, working these big machines.

Working in a mine also meant he doubled his income. But after eight months the miners went on strike during their collective agreement negotiations and it lasted a month. Darcy hadn't been in a union before, the scaffolders being un-unionised.

I was part of the union and we had to go on strike. There was a bit of animosity between the contractors and Solid Energy. When me and Brendon [his mate] went to join the picket line I wasn't sure what the Solid Energy guys [miners] thought, but after that they started to talk to us more. They appreciated us going.

When I ask him the difference between mining and scaffolding he replies: 'The men are different. I think the men here [on the Coast], a good percentage, come from a mining history, mining families, grandfathers, fathers … The history of mining down here is massive. Scaffolding hasn't got that history.'

It took a while, but now he feels accepted. There were rumours that Geotech was on the way out so he moved across to McConnell Dowell, the company that develops the stone drives. He's completed a variety of qualifications and will this year complete his gas ticket, which will make him a qualified miner, capable of leading a group of men underground.

When I ask him about unionism he replies that 'the unions are there to make sure the workers don't get screwed over by the big company'. I ask if that resonates more widely politically and he explains that politics wasn't part of his family when he was growing up, so it's difficult for him to talk about it. But in a perfect society

there would be no racism, everyone would be equal and everyone given a chance, like in the union. Everyone should be able to get educated and get qualified … If we all started running things on the Coast how they run things underground, it would be a lot different. They would think more of the people who do things, the ones who work with their hands, the workers.

For Darcy, life down here is good. They have their house, the work is interesting and well paid, they've managed to buy new vehicles and household goods and he can go fishing and hunting. The sacrifice has been leaving family and friends and living in a less multicultural society. This has been harder on his partner, who hasn't managed to make any close friends her own age here. But they'll put up with that, have a family, she'll home school for a while, and once the mortgage is paid off they may shift back to the city for the children's secondary education. In order to achieve that, Darcy will inevitably work for a period in a mine overseas. He is proud that, despite dropping out of school, he is now a qualified, well-paid worker, in demand globally.

Bang, crackle, pop

Dennis Whata comes from Rotorua and is of Te Arawa and Te Whānau Apanui descent.[68] He was brought up on the family farm, which began as a returned serviceman's land grant. It was a close whānau and in the holidays everyone worked on the land. In return they got their meat from the farm. He reached fifth form at high school but didn't succeed academically because of 'stuff happening', mainly deaths within the family. He had a few jobs before joining the navy at 18, where he was trained as a breech block gunner. He stayed in the navy for 20 years, met his wife who was a navy medic, and they have two children.

He was generally happy in the navy, and the overseas trips were an eye-opener – 'to see how people lived in different countries'. He was on the frigate that supported the Allied effort in the Gulf War, was there for Operation Enduring Freedom (the Iraq war) and joined the NATO force in East Timor. He didn't gain a sense of the political issues, except that if you can do a small job well, that can make a difference. The New Zealand forces were generally in a support capacity rather than on the front line.

But after 20 years it was time for a change – time to move aside and let the next generation move in. 'Our ride had come to an end. We had to make room for other people.' His wife had cousins on the West Coast and his grandmother had whakapapa to the local tangata whenua. They bought a lifestyle block south of Greymouth, built a house and came down in 2009.

He got a job at the freezing works but with the seasonality the pay was too variable. Then a neighbour arranged a job for him with McConnell Dowell. For Dennis, being underground is no different to being on a ship. 'You've got nowhere else to go. Put the lights off on the ship, it's black. You're in a confined space. Same thing. Everything that goes bang, crackle, pop doesn't bother me. I was used to it in the navy – you know, gunfire.'

He loves mining. 'Something different to do all the time, using the machines, good bunch of blokes, pretty tight crew.' He loves the lack of traffic jams on the Coast, 'and then there's the hunting and fishing. Go down the back where I live and you find deer and pigs. The rivers are full of trout. Plus the pace. Up home, go, go, go. Down here, Okay, mate, what're we up to today?'

He misses the whānau, but they're only two hours away by plane and he has a sister in Christchurch. 'If I need a whānau injection, I go over there, see her and the young fullas, have a quick fix.'

Being Māori on the Coast is different from up north:

> I think they're different down here because they look at you differ-ent. I mean up north, I think most people are used to it. Down here Māori are a novelty, unless you're one of those fair-looking Māori. I mean people wouldn't even know with them. Down here – I mean, look at the colour of my skin. They think, he's like one of those fullas on the TV.

In the mine he is reported as being very assertive if anyone makes racist comments, and he pulls people up on their mispronunciation of Māori place names. He's just joined the union, and because of being in the navy has no background in unionism.

> Didn't have a union in the navy. If you had a union no one would go to war. You do what you're told in the navy. Just being away from the military environment is different – it's taken me a while to adjust. In the military, if that's the job in hand, you go and do the job. That's it. None of this sitting around and moaning. If you're a civilian, you can say, Oh, what am I doing this for? I had a lot to learn … A guy from

the EPMU [Engineering, Printing and Manufacturing Union] came and talked to us. There were three of us not in the union. I asked Darcy and he said, Yeah, mate, I'm in the union. He told me about the strike. They help you out. They help you get things.

In the past Dennis has voted Labour ('Auntie Helen'), but then changed to the Māori Party. Now he is considering going back to Labour – except Auntie Helen isn't there any longer. He considers that the activist Māori have the right to their point of view and he is related to some of them; for example, Annette Sykes is his cousin. As for many Māori, politics is bound up with family and iwi.

The activist tradition

Trevor Bolderson is in his fifties and three years ago he migrated from Britain to work at Spring Creek.[69] As a young man he experienced the bitter 1984–85 miners' strike during which Prime Minister Margaret Thatcher took on the coalminers, describing them as 'the enemy within'. He experienced violent clashes with police, the closure of most mines and the demise of traditional mining communities. He worked alongside Arthur Scargill (the famous miners' leader) and remains a traditional left-winger.

When the family came to New Zealand he promised his wife he wouldn't get involved in union politics, but very quickly he became delegate at Spring Creek and is now an influential figure in the local union movement. Watching him in action at a union meeting is very impressive – seeing the respect and authority he carries, with the men and in his dealings with management.

For Trevor there is continuity with 1908.

Back to paradise

David (Digger) Howden is in his forties.[70] He was born in Blackball and his father worked in the Blackball mine, then at Dobson and Rewanui after Blackball closed. Digger remembers Blackball as a mining town (the mine closed when he was five years old):

We had a gang of six or seven of us kids who used to play everywhere – up in the coal bins, in the old tailings down the back, in the old mine. We'd go up to the old Roa mine. I remember we stole all the copper wire when it finished up. The viaduct used to still be there. We'd throw rocks at the streetlights as well. Nothing serious. Gold used to be another hobby. Years ago we could drive over to the back flats across Fords Creek. Dad used to take me gold-panning over there. I still go. Good gold. Good hunting around there as well.

When he left school he worked in forestry, then as a fisherman, before going to Australia to work in the goldmines as a diesel fitter. But over there was hard: 'There's no bush, Everything's dead.' He returned to New Zealand after almost getting blown up on the job, and worked on the roads in Nelson before coming back to Blackball to work at Roa mine, which he loves because of its traditional mining techniques.

We're an old-fashioned mine. We use compressed air and water, that's it. At Spring Creek you get driven to the face and you've got places to have your smoko. At Roa we sit on a pile of coal. We hand bore with six-foot steels. The water pours down so you're soaking wet. You just do a couple of metres at a time. You bolt and mesh it up as you go. You put up props just as an indicator of the weight coming on.

He also loves being back in Blackball.

This place is paradise. You can go fishing, get a deer, go gold-panning, there are three pubs, you've got your mates you work with. I can go out in the bush. I like going gold-panning. There'll be bush robins just about sitting on my hands. It's brilliant. Get back to nature. Living in Blackball you can go and pee out the back door. You can't do that in the city.

It also means he can keep an eye on his elderly parents and help them out with firewood and the like. Digger has always been a union man and he expresses the fundamental value of collectivism with precision: 'Well, you're with everyone. And if something happens and you're against the bosses, you've got something to come back to. You can't get sacked through provocation or whatever.'

Politically, he is equally clear:

The Labour Party stuffed up the country by selling off the assets, forestry etc. It was being run wrong. There were too many chiefs.

> In my forestry gang there were three leading hands in a gang of six.
> Then there were another four bosses above you. Instead of selling it,
> they should have weeded it out and run it properly.

But National he says is on the side of the rich. About the last lot of tax cuts he had this to say: 'It should've been the low-income people got the money. I mean giving the rich another $11,000 is not going to keep them in New Zealand. If they're going for the big money they're gonna go.'

Like Les Neilson, Digger feels he is in political limbo.

Conclusions?

Comparing the 1908 miner and the modern miner, there are similarities and obvious differences. There are still many migrants coming to fill the positions – that is common to both worlds. Now it is a job in which a non-academic person can become a sought-after, well-paid global worker. Back then it was a low-paid casual job, low on the social scale, yet still global because of the skill required. The early 1900s was a period of socialist activity, but now many coal workers are in a state of political limbo. Yet the union remains a strong influence, and there are still activists from outside coming in.

There was a middle period: a 30-year-long Keynesian period (1940–70) during which the mines were state owned, when coalminers formed a 'tribe' or 'guild', with father following son, when family and town life were felt to be stable, when the union was compulsory and virtually ran the town, and when Labour as a political party was closely bonded with the working class.

Perhaps there has been a steady transition, as social and economic life changed, from one state to another, with breaks and continuities but with a key difference being that in both the early and middle periods miners were politically clear and influential in national politics. Whereas the modern miner on the Coast, thanks to the Labour Party's buying into neo-liberalism, is in limbo politically, and because of past betrayals can be tempted to vote for renegade parties like New Zealand First or even, because of income, National or ACT, in line with middle-class interests.

The union's task then is to constantly proselytise regarding the virtues of unionism, to teach a wider sympathy with the cause of low-paid workers and an awareness of the national and international political climate on union operations and working-class interests more generally, and to encourage an international workforce to see themselves in an international union perspective. This task must be undertaken in order to avoid miners becoming a privileged, self-centred and isolated part of the workforce. Interestingly enough, it is not dissimilar to the educational task of the early 1900s.

As well, there is the task of effectively ritualising and teaching mining heritage in order to constantly integrate the modern experience with the rich history. In Britain this has become fundamental in mining towns that have become totally de-industrialised, so that even physical reminders of the past have disappeared. In New Zealand, at this stage, there is still continuity; still a chance to link past and future.

The Pike River disaster, as heritage in the making, has sharply focused these issues.

CHAPTER SEVEN

Dreaming?

It has been a beautiful spring day and in the evening I take a break from perusing the latest transcripts of the Pike River Royal Commission hearing. I make a cup of tea and sit outside. The neighbours are busy, taking advantage of the lengthening days. There is a soundtrack of lawnmowers, hammering, a distant chainsaw, the determined bleat of lambs, and of course the birds are busy.

I admire the new tunnel-house we put up last weekend and remember Kevin Hague's dream of turning coal into carbon fibre. We now have a few cubic metres of the subtropics in our back yard. How neat an equation that would have been, for the tunnel-house to have been made from the carbon captured and stored by those trees 200 million years ago, thus continuing their task of making the planet a more fertile place.

The Pike transcripts don't make easy reading. Hamlet would have had a field day with the Polonius-type phrases of those in charge of the rescue operation: 'significant gaps in the information space'; 'permissive operating environment'; 'an individual who has an ultimate layer of responsibility'; 'dynamic risk assessment based on the safe person concept'; 'decisions or wilful actions'; 'due diligence and scrutiny' …

A dumbshow is called for, instead of these countless hours of fudging the obvious. 'O what a piece of work is man.' Like Hamlet, a person could become cynical.

There is still an hour or so of light. Children clatter down the road, dragging along some new contraption with that inspired enthusiasm that the young have.

I return to Badiou. The task of this book, rather than to descend into cynicism, has been to name this event, to see it evolve for a moment in a consistent way and to glimpse the future.

Kevin Hague, who has mining in his whakapapa (an uncle was killed at Strongman), believes that an important cultural task on the West Coast is to take the values of our mining heritage (solidarity, collective responsibility, camaraderie) into the new era.

And that is beginning to happen.

Environmentalists realise there are workers and communities affected when industrial activities are curtailed, and have introduced a concept of just transition into their thinking. Similarly, those of a socialist persuasion have had to take into account the central importance of environmental issues.

From this duet is coming a new movement that has acquired an exponential energy. The coal-tar sands pipeline protest in Washington resulted in more arrests than any other protest since the Vietnam war. Then it moved into an occupation of Wall Street.

In any such movement that will, à la Badiou, be characterised by multiplicity, one finds a niche that appeals. I am particularly taken by the Awakening the Dreamer movement, which arose from interaction between rainforest activists and Amazonian indigenous peoples.[71] The tribal elders said to the activists, 'Go back to your people and tell them to dream a different dream.' It is a simple yet profound concept, based on the notion that we dream the world.

The dream that has led us to the brink of environmental catastrophe is the dream of constant expansion, constant growth, increased consumption, ever faster technological change, ever greater manipulation of natural resources and life systems, increased levels of performance in every facet of our work and social life, the market as the 'neutral controller' …

It is a dream that oppresses. I came down here to try to get away from it.

The sun drifts below the Paparoas and the air chills.

What different dream might we begin to dream that contains the three core values of this movement: sustainability, social justice, spiritual health?

Let us start with a society where major projects will have state input, worker input and their capital base judged secure before they go ahead; a society where work takes place in a health and safety regulatory framework that has company, state and worker involvement.

Māori and Pākehā on the Coast will work through the perceived Treaty of Waitangi and other betrayals in order to achieve a bicultural and future-oriented society.

It is a society in which the miners and their union will be conscious of their heritage and the historical role they have played in this country and this region, and they will return to being a force for social justice at all levels.

The mining sector, including the workforce and their union, will have its own environmental vision regarding coal and its uses and the rate at which we mine the resource, from which to negotiate with tangata whenua, environmentalists and regional representatives.

A transition economy will be an important part of this vision, with Development West Coast focusing its resources on this task. Coasters will see that in order to achieve the transition, the nation – and the wider world – need to move away from market-driven neo-liberalism, and the region will join with others who are actively seeking this.

In a discrete regional community these reasonable and indeed pragmatic goals should be achievable. This is not utopianism, except for those locked into the mainstream. The new dream can be dreamed. For it should be waking reality.

There are 29 bodies, 29 family histories, trapped in the ground, in a national park, interrupting the flow of capital. The international unions line up with the local union and the families, demanding recovery. It is a potent symbol. Those buried in the mountain have become prophets of the future.

It is beginning to be dusk and the dog requires a walk so I take her down the hill, through the beech forest to the creek. A kereru flies past, signalling the coming summer. In winter they go deep into the bush, before returning to the village to feed off the budding manuka, broom and willow. They are not purists.

I walk along the creek bed, recently re-formed by a goldminer. He had developed a level track along the creek and left us a swimming hole, but a recent flood destroyed his careful work in a day. Now we are back to a rough and tumbled landscape.

This creek bed has been dug over many times: by hand, by dredge, by digger.

Finally, perhaps, it will be left in peace.

In which case, in 20 years it will appear untouched.

ENDNOTES

1   Subcomandante Marcos, Zapatista Army of National Liberation, Mexico, *Our Word is our Weapon*, New York: Seven Stories Press, 2001.
2   Alain Badiou, *Being and Event* (trs. Oliver Feltham), New York: Continuum, 2005.
3   Throughout this book neo-liberalism is taken as the ideology behind the 'revolution' that began in New Zealand in 1984. Jane Kelsey summarises the key factors in *Reclaiming the Future* (Wellington: Bridget Williams Books, 1999): 'Treasury's answer to New Zealand's "serious macroeconomic policy imbalances" was a textbook application of neo-liberal economic theory. Government should adopt a monetarist approach to controlling inflation, and float the currency. The labour market had to be deregulated, and protections removed from industry and agriculture. Tighter controls on government spending were required, accompanied by a shift towards indirect taxation and commercialisation of the public sector and social policy.'
4   Barbara Freese, *Coal: A human history*, London: Arrow Books, 2005, pp. 233–34.
5   Len Richardson, *Coal, Class & Community: The United Mineworkers of New Zealand, 1880–1960*, Auckland: Auckland University Press, 1995.
6   First published in *Arena* magazine, no. 110, March 2011, pp. 19–24.
7   Jean Baudrillard, *Screened Out* (trs. Chris Turner), London/New York: Verso, 2002.
8   Freese, *Coal: A human history*, p. 73.
9   Ibid., p. 75.
10 Even for a modern mine like Pike River the transport issue was complex, initially provoking an environmental debate when it was proposed to truck the coal to Greymouth at the rate of a truck every 10 minutes, 24 hours a day. Eventually a more sensible rail option was negotiated with Solid Energy.
11 Karl Marx and Frederick Engels, *Selected Works*, Moscow: Progress Publishers, 1969, p. 137.
12 See Kate Bowan and Paul A. Pickering, 'Singing for socialism', in Laurajane Smith, Paul A. Shackel and Gary Campbell (eds), *Heritage, Labour and the*

Working Classes, New York/London: Routledge, 2011, pp. 192–216.

13 'Solidarity For Ever', written by Industrial Workers of the World (IWW) poet and organiser Ralph Chaplin for a hunger march in Chicago in 1915.

14 James Belich, *Making Peoples: A history of the New Zealanders from Polynesian settlement to the end of the nineteenth century*, Auckland: Penguin, 1996.

15 Richardson, *Coal, Class & Community*, p. 8.

16 Ibid., p. 9.

17 Ibid., p. 52.

18 Ibid., p. 85.

19 Eric Beardsley, *Blackball '08*, Auckland: Collins, 1984.

20 Paul Maunder, *On Yer Bike*, first performed in Blackball, Mayday 2005, subsequently at Regent Theatre, Greymouth, as part of the centenary, Easter 2008.

21 From the union anthem 'The Red Flag', by Jim Connell, 1889.

22 Richardson, *Coal, Class & Community*, p. 96.

23 Ibid., p. 112.

24 Constitution of the Zealand Federation of Miners, p. 306.

25 In 2005, when Labour Minister Trevor Mallard was closing down schools in the Grey District, I persuaded locals to repeat the action. Blackball School remains.

26 Michael King, *The Penguin History of New Zealand*, Auckland: Penguin Books, 2003; Richard Hill, *The Iron Fist in the Velvet Glove: The modernisation of policing in New Zealand 1886–1917*, Palmerston North: Dunmore Press, 1995.

27 Richardson, *Coal, Class & Community*, p. 148.

28 Ibid., p. 150.

29 Ibid., p. 151.

30 Forty-three men were killed in an explosion on the Waikato coalfields, revealing once again deficiencies in the policing of coalmine regulations.

31 Richardson, *Coal, Class & Community*, p. 130.

32 Ibid., p. 174.

33 Ibid., p. 308.

34 Ibid., p. 224.

35 Ibid., p. 298.

36 Ross Wilson, 'Workplace heath and safety laws in New Zealand: For whose benefit?' *Labour History Project Newsletter*, March 2011.

37 www.dol.govt.nz/consultation/underground-mining/index.asp (accessed 7 July 2011).

38 www.pikeriver.royalcommission.govt.nz: transcript, Monday 11 July.

39 www.pikeriver.royalcommission.govt.nz: transcript, Tuesday, 12 July.

40 www.pikeriver.royalcommission.govt.nz: transcript, Wednesday, 13 July.

41 Wolfgang Rosenberg, *New Zealand Can be Different and Better*, Christchurch: New Zealand Monthly Review Society, 1993.

42 Raymond Williams, *The Year 2000*, New York: Pantheon Books, 1983, pp. 140–41.

43 Guy Debord, *The Society of the Spectacle* (trs. Donald Nicholson-Smith), New York: Zone Books, 1995, p. 13.

44 Ibid., p. 14.

45 Les Neilson, personal interview, 13 July 2011.

46 Available at www.homepages.caverock.net.nz/~bj/beech.

47   www.nzine.co.nz/features/timberlands1.html.
48   Nicky Hager, *Secrets and Lies*, Nelson: Craig Potton Publishing, 1999.
49   Available at www.converge.org.nz/nfa/history2.htm.
50   There is a further irony here, in that humping and hollowing effectively buries the beech seed that lies in Coast soil, and which had previously meant that beech forest would grow on any land left idle. Rick Barber (Makaawhio) believes humping and hollowing is the 'final colonisation'.
51   See Richard Fahey (ed), *Clay Economies*, Auckland: Six Point Press, 2008.
52   The Westland and Nelson Native Reserves Act 1887.
53   www.waitangi-tribunal.govt.nz/Ngai Tahu Report.
54   'The trouble with Mawhera', *Press*, 18 January 2008.
55   See for example www.nzherald.co.nz/greymouth/news/article.cfm?l_id=205.
56   Zero Emissions Platform, 'The costs of CO_2 capture, transport and storage': www.zeroemissionproject.com (accessed 20 July 2011).
57   See www.worldcoal.org/carbon-capture-storage.
58   See www.zeroemissionsplatform.eu.
59   'A shrinking window of opportunity for CCS in Europe?': www.ifandp.com (accessed 7 July 2011).
60   Freese, *Coal: A human history*, pp. 264–65.
61   Victoria University of Wellington, Institute for Policy Studies, Coal Symposium, 27 May 2011: www.ips.ac.nz/events/downloads/2011/CoalSymposium_2011.
62   See Don Elder's evidence: www.pikeriverroyalcommission.govt.org/transcript: 11 July 2011.
63   Les Neilson, personal interview, 13 July 2011.
64   Kevin Hague, personal interview, 7 September 2011.
65   Smith et al, *Heritage, Labour and the Working Classes*, p. 3.
66   Ibid., Chapter 5.
67   Darcy Tuiavi'i, personal interview, 30 May 2011.
68   Dennis Whata, personal interview, 7 June 2011.
69   'United we stand', *Greymouth Star*, 2 November 2010.
70   David (Digger) Howden, personal interview, 12 September 2010.
71   www.awakeningthedreamer.org.

Anon. 'A shrinking window of opportunity for CCS in Europe?':
www.ifandp.com (accessed 7 July 2011)

Badiou, Alain. *Being and Event* (trs. Oliver Feltham), New York:
Continuum, 2005

Baudrillard, Jean. *Screened Out* (trs. Chris Turner), London/New York:
Verso, 2002

Beardsley, Eric. *Blackball '08*, Auckland: Collins, 1984

Belich, James. *Making Peoples: A history of the New Zealanders from
Polynesian settlement to the end of the nineteenth century*, Auckland:
Penguin, 1996

Debord, Guy. *The Society of the Spectacle* (trs. Donald Nicholson-Smith),
New York: Zone Books, 1995

Elder, Don. Evidence, Pike River Commission of Inquiry: www.
pikeriverroyalcommission.govt.org/transcript, July 11th

Fahey, Richard (ed.). *Clay Economies*, Auckland: Six Point Press, 2008

Freese, Barbara. *Coal: A human history*, London: Arrow Books, 2005

Hager, Nicky. *Secrets and Lies*, Nelson: Craig Potton Publishing, 1999

Hague, Kevin. Personal interview, 7 September 2011

Hill, Richard. *The Iron Hand in the Velvet Glove: The modernisation of
policing in New Zealand, 1886–1917*, Palmerston North: Dunmore
Press, 1995

Howden, David. Personal interview, 12 September 2010

Jesson, Bruce. *Only Their Purpose is Mad: The money men take over New
Zealand*, Palmerston North: Dunmore Press, 1999

Kelsey, Jane. *Reclaiming the Future*, Wellington: Bridget Williams Books
Ltd, 1999

King, Michael. *The Penguin History of New Zealand*, Auckland: Penguin Books, 2003

Marcos, Subcomandante, Zapatista Army of National Liberation, Mexico, *Our Word is our Weapon*, New York: Seven Stories Press, 2001

Marx, Karl and Frederick Engels, *Selected Works*, Moscow: Progress Publishers, 1969

Maunder, Paul. 'Diary of a disaster', *Arena* magazine, March 2011, pp. 19–24

Maunder, Paul. *On Yer Bike*, first performed in Blackball, Mayday 2005, subsequently at Regent Theatre, Greymouth, as part of the centenary, Easter 2008. Script available: www.blackballmuseum.org.nz

Neilson, Les. Personal interview, 13 July 2011

Richardson, Len. *Coal, Class & Community: The United Mineworkers of New Zealand, 1880–1960*, Auckland: Auckland University Press, 1995

Rosenberg, Wolfgang. 'New Zealand can be different and better', *New Zealand Monthly Review*, 1993

Ross, Andrew (ed.). *Universal Abandon? The politics of postmodernism*, Edinburgh: Edinburgh University Press, 1989

Smith, Laurajane, Paul A. Shackel and Gary Campbell (eds), *Heritage, Labour and the Working Classes*, New York/London: Routledge, 2011

Tuiavi'i, Darcy. Personal interview, 30 May 2011

Victoria University of Wellington, Institute for Policy Studies, Coal Symposium, 27 May 2011: www.ips.ac.nz/events/downloads/2011/CoalSymposium_2011

Whata, Dennis. Personal interview, 7 June 2011

Williams, Raymond. *The Year 2000*, New York: Pantheon Books, 1983

Wilson, Ross. 'Workplace heath and safety laws in New Zealand: For whose benefit?' *Labour History Project Newsletter*, March 2011

Zero Emissions Platform, 'The costs of CO_2 capture, transport and storage': www.zeroemissionproject.com (accessed 20 July 2011)

www.converge.org.nz/nfa/history2.htm

www.dol.govt.nz/consultation/underground-mining/index.asp (accessed 7 July 2011)

www.homepages.caverock.net.nz/~bj/beech

www.nzherald.co.nz/greymouth/news/article.cfm?l_id=205

www.nzine.co.nz/features/timberlands1.html

www.waitangi-tribunal.govt.nz/Ngai Tahu Report

www.worldcoal.org/carbon-capture-storage

www.zeroemissionsplatform.eu

hongi	to press noses in greeting
kaupapa	agenda, guiding principles
Papatūānuku	Mother Earth
pounamu	greenstone, jade
rūnanga	council
tangata whenua	first people of the land
tiriti	treaty
tūrangawaewae	place to stand, home
whakapapa	genealogy
whānau	extended family